What to do when you want to give up

Help for entrepreneurs in tough times

Allon Raiz

with

Trevor Waller

BOOK**STORM** MACMILLAN

Dedication

To Sunet Wagner – perseverance personified

ISBN: 978-1-920434-32-8

First edition, first impression 2012

Published jointly by Bookstorm (Pty) Limited and
Pan Macmillan (Pty) Limited

Bookstorm (Pty) Limited
Suite 10
Private Bag X12
Cresta 2118
Johannesburg
South Africa

Pan Macmillan (Pty) Limited
Private Bag X19
Northlands 2116
South Africa

Distributed by Pan Macmillan
via Booksite Afrika

Edited by Mark Ronan
Proofread by John Henderson
Cover design by Karin Barry-McCormack
Book design Lebone Publishing Services
Typeset by Lebone Publishing Services
Printed and bound by Ultra Litho (Pty) Limited

Contents

Acknowledgements vi

Introduction 1

Chapter 1:   Passion and pain 3

Chapter 2:   Does your business have an
             economic right to exist? 15

Chapter 3:   Do you have non-financial
             resources to tap into? 60

Chapter 4:   Can you do something else in order
             to bring in cash? 84

Chapter 5:   Do you believe in your abilities?   99

Chapter 6:   Are you thinking big enough? ... 113

Chapter 7:   What are you missing? 132

Chapter 8:   Sell, sell, sell 157

Epilogue   175

References   178

Acknowledgements

Although this book is based on a true story, the character of Rachel is really a composite of many of the entrepreneurs whom I have had the privilege to engage with and guide during my journey in Raizcorp. The common thread among them all is their ability to persevere through the toughest of times. Their attitude and mindset continue to be an inspiration to me.

To Sunet Wagner who, with her husband, Werner, came to meet with me that fateful Saturday – you are a beacon of light to all entrepreneurs who are going through their own struggles. You are blessed with what we at Raizcorp call blue heart – the heart of an entrepreneur. Never ever give up.

To all my Raizcorp partner companies who are mentioned directly or indirectly in the story, thank you for the permission to use your stories in the book.

To my Entrepreneurs' Organisation Forum members: Tim White, Rich Mulholland, Angel Jones, Wanda Shuenyane, Kumaran Padayachee, Robert Dennison, JP Villion, Randal Wahl and Mark Levy, thank you for all the support and wisdom you have given me through my entrepreneurial journey. You have been there to support me through some really rough times.

To my business partner Colin Kapeluschnik, thank you for your patience, once again, while I wrote this book. It's complete, but I cannot ever promise you that it will be the last one.

To my wife, Toni, and my two boys, Cannen and Denim, thank you for your unwavering support and for sacrificing so many weekends so that I could complete this book. Toni, thank you for reading through the manuscript again and again and again. I am grateful for your insights and our debates.

To my two good friends Alfie Naidoo and Kumaran Padayachee, who gave invaluable feedback during the editing process. Thank you for your time and commitment to this project. Your perspectives and single malt are highly appreciated.

And, finally, to Trevor Waller, my co-author: I am blessed to have someone like you in my life. We have such a special working relationship that often resembles two old men grumbling at each other on the park bench. The end result is magic.

Introduction

This book is based on the true story of an entrepreneur who, despite the obvious signs that her business was about to turn and flourish, chose to give up. However, before making her final decision, I suggested she spend a day with me to interrogate whether her reasons for wanting to give up were valid. One day led to another, which led to a series of encounters which allowed her to make a better-informed, less emotional decision.

Many people do not know how many times I also thought of giving up on my dream. And like many of you who are reading this book, I too faced a really dire financial situation.

You will understand the pain of borrowing money from your family. You know what that does to your self-image. You know the shameful feeling of borrowing money from your friends. I even remember, in a moment of absolute despair, plucking up the courage to ask my father's friend to lend me money. He said no; I was devastated.

I think that even worse than asking to borrow money, even worse than the anxiety before the meeting, and the knot in your stomach just before you ask, is the feeling of being rejected and declined. It's the feeling that guys get when they have been deliberating all night whether to ask the prettiest girl out on a date, and she rejects them. Sometimes she even laughs and tells her friends.

What do you do when all the financial indicators are telling you that you are a failure, but a voice deep inside (sometimes too deep) is telling you that you have something special? When do you know whether you are conning yourself, or if indeed there is something worthwhile there? How do you handle the disparity between what you portray to the world and what is really going on inside? It takes so much energy to keep up that facade.

I remember the strategies I used when I had meetings with people. I would invite someone for coffee and not order anything myself so that they would feel obliged to pay. Of course, I would offer. I prayed that the meeting would result in some imminent business as I walked back to my car, pulled out the ten 50-cent pieces I had collected that morning from an old change bottle in my cupboard and paid the parking attendant. Sometimes I cried as I drove back to the office, with the petrol gauge on empty. And one day there came a point of so much pain that I literally collapsed onto the floor in my newly born child's room. I could not carry on any more. Decisions needed to be made.

Written as a series of conversations between me and Rachel, a struggling entrepreneur, this book looks at the issues facing entrepreneurs who are asking themselves:

- ■ Do I admit defeat or do I carry on?
- ■ Do I find a way to build my business or do I get a job?
- ■ Do I follow my head or my heart?

CHAPTER 1

Passion and pain

The meeting

By the time we scheduled our meeting, Rachel was ready to throw in the towel. She had started her design business, Divine Designs, three years earlier, watched it grow and watched it shrink. And grow again. And dip again. On the morning that we met, Rachel had had enough. The strain of the perpetual ups and downs that accompany the entrepreneurial journey was beginning to show. I understood Rachel's position. I had been there and I had seen many others in the same place. I offered to meet her, in Raizcorp's boardroom, on a Saturday. There would be little disruption, and, although I hoped to be home by late afternoon, I was prepared to go beyond if necessary. My personal assistant, Naz, had arranged enough coffee, tea and snacks to keep us going.

There is very little I will not do to help an entrepreneur stay the course. I take a decidedly pro-life view when it comes to entrepreneurs and their businesses. Unless both are dead, I prefer to find ways to help them survive! Helping Rachel to keep her business alive was my mission for the day.

Despite my 'pro-life' stance, however, I have worked with enough entrepreneurs to know that sometimes the decision to give up may indeed be the right one. However, giving up needs to be a considered decision:

the entrepreneur cannot give up simply because the journey is hard. Too often, when something is 'hard', we convince ourselves that it is 'wrong'. Hard and wrong are not the same thing. If Rachel is to give up, it must be because this particular business – at this particular time – is wrong, not because it is hard to keep going. Very few successful entrepreneurs speak of an easy road. That is why resilience is a defining feature of entrepreneurs.

I invited Rachel to bring her husband, Steve, to the meeting. Although not an entrepreneur himself, Steve had been at Rachel's side from the beginning of her entrepreneurial journey. With his charming ability to be both strong and gentle at the same time, Steve had supported Rachel in giving up her job and risking their savings on her business. Design was Rachel's passion, and Steve had been happy for her to find ways to employ her passion in the pursuit of a profitable business. Now he was losing patience and his hope was dwindling. Steve, ever the optimist, was now looking decidedly dejected but his presence at the meeting was important. He knew Rachel better than anyone and I trusted that he would be honest enough to help her make a decision that was right for her now. Put simply, the decision facing Rachel was, should she carry on or should she give it all up? Whatever decision she was to make, Rachel would need Steve's support.

That feeling of deep emptiness

The Raizcorp boardroom is not a large room. It has a wooden table that can comfortably seat eight people. In the middle of the table is a collection of small toys: Lego blocks, plastic alphabet letters, toy cars, some balls and a few mini-puzzle pieces. The toys signal that this is not a corporate boardroom; it is an entrepreneurial space. The toys remind us that although we are at work, we also need to be having fun. When entrepreneurs stop having fun, they begin to lose hope. The toys are a reminder: no matter how hard it gets, dig deep and find the fun again. I began by asking Rachel to choose a toy that she believed represented herself at this stage. Looking at the toys, she reached out and picked up a small, orange ping-pong ball. Fascinated by her choice, I enquired why she had chosen the table tennis ball. Rolling the ball across the table, she let it fall to the floor.

'That's me,' she said. 'Right now, I have no power. I may look solid, even strong,' she laughed, 'but inside I'm empty.'

I said nothing, letting Rachel continue. 'I can't actually do anything until someone pushes me and, right now, all I want to do is lie on the floor and be left alone.'

As I listened, I couldn't help think back to my first encounter with Rachel. I had just finished giving a talk to a group of would-be entrepreneurs when she bounced up to me. She was gutsy, determined and glowing. The sparkle in her eye told me that she had just the right mixture of excitement and trepidation to make it with her own business. Had I been wrong? I hoped not.

Steve had been quiet all this time. 'Which object would you choose for Rachel?' I asked him.

'That's easy,' he replied, picking up a toy sports car. 'Rachel is as powerful as this car,' he said. 'She just needs a service,' he joked. 'That's why we're here today.' He hesitated, before tentatively adding, 'We need to help Rachel get back her power, I think.' His eyes moistened. Rachel, I knew, was in a room with two men whose sole intention was to give her the space and love she needed to reclaim her power to make a decision that was right for her. She reached over to take Steve's hand. It is so easy to forget that, for every entrepreneur who is failing or succeeding, there are many other people, in the background, deeply affected by the highs and lows that are the inevitable result of one person trying to build a business.

The passion test

'Right,' I said, 'enough playing around. Let's get serious.'

We helped ourselves to coffee and muffins, and I decided to jump straight in. 'Tell me,' I asked Rachel, 'What would you be doing if you weren't running your current business?'

She did not reply immediately, and I could see that she was thinking deeply. She reached for Steve's hand again and, finally, she said, 'I don't know. I can't answer that question. There is nothing else I want to be doing.' She looked at me sheepishly. 'You see, I am a ping-pong ball. I can't even answer your question.'

'You answered that question perfectly,' I said.

'What do you mean?' she asked, looking at me quizzically.

I stood up, walked over to the whiteboard, and picked up a marker. I drew a circle in the middle of the board and, inside the circle, I wrote one word: 'passion'.

I looked directly into Rachel's eyes. 'This is great news. If you had given me any answer other than "nothing", we would really be in trouble,' I told her. 'When I ask entrepreneurs what they would rather be doing, many of them express a desire to be doing something else; they would rather be in another business, even another industry. This disappoints me deeply. This tells me that these entrepreneurs are not following their passion. And I believe that when an entrepreneur is not building his business in something he is passionate about, he is destined for trouble.'

Rachel's choice of a ping-pong ball to represent her current state of being was extremely telling. The lightweight ball is hollow. The emptiness Rachel was feeling is something I have witnessed in many entrepreneurs who find themselves in a situation where there seems to be little forward motion in their business. I meet these entrepreneurs all the time. I call them the 'seeker entrepreneurs'. They attend the talks, the workshops, the courses and the conferences. They buy the books and search the web. They find others like themselves. They become addicted to the search, looking everywhere for input. The one place they forget to look is inside. Today, whether she knew it or not, Rachel was going to have to look deep inside herself.

While I was willing to pose questions, tell stories and share insights, ultimately I knew that the only way Rachel could make her decision was to choose a path that was true for her.

Passion is not necessarily passion

It has become almost a cliché that entrepreneurs need passion, and so I asked Rachel to tell me what exactly her passion is.

'I'm passionate about design,' was her response.

'Tell me why,' I said.

A broad smile crossed her face. 'I've always loved drawing and I love giving people something beautiful to look at, something that inspires them,' she said. The upbeat tone of her voice made it clear that she was not just saying the words. She continued, 'I love creating things and giving expression to ideas in a visual way. When I turn an idea, or even an emotion, into a picture, it feels as if I am turning a dream into reality. I make ideas solid, turning them into something that people can see and feel and hold.'

She sat back, looking proud of her ability to express her passion.

'So what you are actually passionate about is not design,' I said. 'If I understand you correctly, your passion is giving expression to ideas.'

'That's it!' she said excitedly. 'And it's exactly what my business allows me to do.'

'In that case, you pass the passion test,' I said to Rachel. 'And the fact that, even now, at your lowest point, there is nothing you would rather be doing, tells me that your passion is aligned to what you are doing. That is the first crucial ingredient for success.'

Rachel smiled. It was her first real smile of the day. In arranging the meetings, I had told Rachel to bring a portfolio of her work, as well as a notebook with her. There would be a lot of discussion and, I suspected, a lot of emotion. I did not want the information to get lost in the emotion. I was glad to see that Rachel was beginning to use her notebook. I glanced down and saw that she had written the following on the first page of her notebook:

PASSION – GIVING EXPRESSION TO IDEAS

Commitment trumps passion

'Do you mind if I ask the two of you a very personal question?' I asked, looking at Steve and Rachel.

'Of course not,' said Steve immediately.

Rachel looked a little less enthusiastic. We had worked together many times and she knew that I have a propensity to go where angels fear to tread.

'How long have you been married?' I asked.

'Ten years,' came Rachel's quick reply.

'Tell me honestly,' I said, 'How different is your marriage now from ten years ago?'

Rachel blushed and Steve looked down at the desk.

'You don't have to answer,' I said. 'We all know the answer because, like all humans, we know that, while passion may be what attracts us to each other, it is commitment that keeps us together.'

'We still love each other!' said Steve.

'I have no doubt of that,' I said. 'Just as I have no doubt that Rachel still loves her business. But the initial euphoria – the heart that beats fast when you first meet the love of your life, or first open the business you have always dreamt of – that euphoria cannot last. Keeping it alive takes work. That is the work of commitment. Commitment is passion's twin, but it is the neglected child.' I stood up and drew a second circle on the board. In this circle, I wrote 'commitment'.

'I'm committed,' said Rachel, 'but I'm also tired. I'm tired and weary,' she said. 'Of course you are,' I said, smiling.

'But your passion and commitment are what give you the ability to persevere, and we know that perseverance is what it's all about. Every successful person has experienced fatigue along the way. But they dig deep, they commit and they continue to act in pursuit of their dreams.'

Suddenly, Rachel burst into tears. I remained silent. I have worked with enough entrepreneurs, not to mention life coaches, not to be afraid of emotion. I expected tears and knew that, on the other side of the tears, would lie the answers that Rachel needed.

Almost every book on entrepreneurship has a chapter dedicated to passion. In fact, knowing that passion is a prerequisite for success, many struggling entrepreneurs will adjust their story so that it looks like their business correlates with their passion. It is more important for entrepreneurs to be honest with themselves and take the time to really understand what it is they are truly passionate about.

If Rachel was passionate about animals, Divine Designs would, most probably, be the wrong business for her. Once entrepreneurs have established their passion, and are sure that their business allows them to fulfil this passion, they need to dig deep in order to keep building their business. Passion may not last; perseverance and commitment must. Perseverance is the ability to keep going, no matter how hard the journey. Commitment is loyalty to your cause. It provides the energy to stay the course.

The entrepreneur's sirens

Eventually, Rachel spoke. 'My friend has offered me a job,' she said. 'I told her I would give her an answer on Monday.'

'Aha! You have a siren in your life!' I said.

Rachel looked confused and asked what I was talking about. She did not know, and so I explained to her that, in Greek mythology, sirens were part-female, part-bird creatures that lived on a rocky island. They sang songs so beautiful that sailors were irresistibly drawn towards them. The sailors would steer their boats so close to the island that they would either hit rocks or they would jump into the water to get closer. They could not resist the lure of the sirens.

Rachel looked even more confused now.

'I know exactly what you're going through,' I said. Rachel sat silently as I continued. 'A few years ago, I was at an entrepreneurial conference in Norway when I got an e-mail from a large bank. I was offered the opportunity to head up a division of the bank. The package was temptingly large and I knew that it would allow me to service my ever-increasing debt – incurred from my own attempts to build a business. Building Raizcorp was difficult and I was taking strain. I spoke to my wife, and endlessly discussed the offer with my friends. Raizcorp's success was not a certainty at that stage, and I really did not know what to do. When I eventually made my decision, it was accompanied by trepidation and self-questioning but I knew that the position at the bank would not allow me to fulfil my passion. For a short while after I had turned it down, I dreamt about what I could have done with the money. But that dream was smaller than the dream I had of building my own business and of assisting others to do the same. That was my passion and I was committed to it,' I said.

When one is feeling particularly vulnerable, as I was then, I explained to her, almost everything is more tempting than one's current situation. My job offer at that time and Rachel's offer then are the sirens of entrepreneurship.

There is no entrepreneurial nirvana, a place where suddenly it is comfortable and easy. The pain does not go away. Rather, it continually changes with circumstances. The pain of not being able to deliver is replaced by the inability to deliver when there are too many. The pain of the former (i.e. no clients) is replaced by the pain of having to implement policies when you hire new staff to service the many clients. And so it continues.

If you do not have both passion and commitment, when the hard times hit you will be susceptible to all sorts of sirens that will distract you on your journey. If, however, you are mission-bound, if what you're doing is following your passion, and your commitment is real, you will find a way to withstand these temptations. Then you are more likely to persevere through the pain, rediscover your passion, recommit to your mission and continue to build your business.

Sometimes, of course, it is the right decision to take the job. Taking the job might be because one knows that entrepreneurship is not for you. Other times, it may simply be a question of timing. You may be an entrepreneur but the time may not be right to launch – or even continue building – your business.

There is no one-size-fits-all answer to the question. I have worked with entrepreneurs for whom the call to 'get a job' is the right one but they feel that their investment in their business is too much for them to give up. Ignoring the siren, they continue to build their business and succeed. Others do not.

One rock at a time

I asked Rachel if she'd seen the film *The Shawshank Redemption*. She hadn't, and so, warning her that I would be spoiling the movie for her, I explained that in the movie Tim Robbins plays Andy Dufresne, a wrongfully convicted prisoner, who spends 20 years digging his way out of prison. Armed with a tiny rock hammer, he chisels his way out of his cell, covering the hole with a poster. With remarkable patience, planning and execution, under the nose of the guards, his prison friends, and even the audience, he wins his freedom. He smiles and grins, and continues tunnelling, taking a little sand at a time and surreptitiously emptying it down inside the leg of his trousers into the courtyard.

'That's great,' said Steve. 'But what does that have to do with us right now?'

Rachel knew. 'I'm Dufresne,' she said.

'Absolutely,' I said, 'You build a business like he builds his escape route. Every action, every phone call, every small deal is a step closer to achieving your dream.' If building your business is your passion, you need the patience and commitment of a convicted prisoner tunnelling his way to freedom. You will let nothing stand in your way.

Checklist for Chapter 1	
Are you passionate about this business?	
Are you committed to this business?	
Can you withstand the pain?	
Can you withstand the temptations?	

CHAPTER 2

Does your business have an economic right to exist?

What are you selling?

We continued our meeting and I began by asking Rachel a question that, on the surface, seems completely self-evident. Yet, it is a question that baffles many an entrepreneur. The question is very simple: 'What do you sell?' Rachel looked at me, her eyes narrowing, as if to say, 'You know very well what I sell; you've bought from me!' We bantered, back and forth, for a few minutes, as Rachel attempted to wriggle out of answering the question.

Allon: So, what do you sell?

Rachel: What do you mean?

Allon: What does your business sell?

Rachel: We sell design.

Allon: What is design?

Rachel: What do you mean? Design is design.

Allon: Who would I be if I was buying design from you?

Rachel: You would be somebody who wanted design work …

Allon: I get that, but I'm not clear as to why your clients are buying it specifically from *you*.

At this point, Rachel began to get visibly irritated. 'I really don't know where you're going with this,' she said.

Steve smiled at me. I wondered if he knew why I was asking these questions.

'What are you working on at the moment?' I asked Rachel.

Rachel proceeded to tell me that she was designing the packaging of a new food range for Woolworths.

'What does your design do for Woolworths?' I asked her.

Rachel looked at me with a puzzled expression. I knew I had to clarify the questions further. 'What would be the difference to Woolworths if you gave them a terrible design, rather than a great one?'

'My great design enables them to sell more products. If I gave them a poor design, they would sell fewer products.'

I looked straight into her eyes. It was vital that she understood what I was about to say. Rachel had to understand the essence of why her clients were buying from her. This understanding was a vital piece of the puzzle that she needed to assemble when making the decision to give up or to continue building her business.

'So, what your clients are buying from you is the ability to sell more products.'

I paused briefly. 'They are *not* buying design,' I said, thumping the table lightly, yet dramatically, hoping that Rachel was finally beginning to get the message.

Rachel's next question, asked almost defensively, made me realise that she might require more persuasion.

'What about the layout of the clothing shop window I just completed?' she asked.

'What is the purpose of a shop window?' came my quick retort.

Rachel hesitated, looking past me. I could see she was thinking deeply about my question.

'I guess it's the same as packaging,' she conceded. 'The shop window attracts customers.'

We continued to investigate Rachel's work. From adverts for pet stores, to brochures for tour operators, to packaging for health food manufacturers, Rachel came to see that almost all her clients were buying her designs in order to increase their sales. It was her designs that they were using in order to attract more customers. Suddenly, Rachel was no longer in the business of selling design. She was selling customer attraction. This was the value she was giving her clients.

> *In my experience, most entrepreneurs don't work hard enough to understand – and articulate – what it is they are really selling.*

Woolworths chose Rachel over her competitors, to do their design work, not necessarily because she was cheaper, but because they believed that her designs had the best ability to attract customers. There is little doubt, however, that other factors also played a role. Price, reputation and even personal relationships could all have been contributing factors. But, ultimately, the main reason that Rachel won the contract is that Woolworths (and all her other clients for that matter) believe that her design will attract more customers, thereby increasing their sales. The ability to attract customers is Rachel's real value to Woolworths. Understanding the value you provide to your clients – i.e. why exactly they buy from you – is vital to growing your business.

Rachel has spent so much time convincing herself, and others, about her ability to design, that she struggles to think of her business as selling anything else. When making the decision to continue or to give up, entrepreneurs need to appreciate what value they are actually providing to their clients. If there is indeed real value, then perhaps giving up is not such a good idea.

The signs of value

'How do we know that the value that Rachel's clients are getting is real?' asked Steve. 'Maybe, they're just using her because she's the cheapest.'

'I am most certainly not cheap!' she said, looking at him indignantly.

He avoided making eye contact with her and looked directly at me, awaiting my response.

I congratulated Steve on his insight.

'So, Rachel,' I asked, 'how do you know that the value is real?'

'Well, Woolworths, for example, has been using me for more than two years,' she said. 'Surely that proves value?'

'It certainly does,' I replied. 'Repeat buying is a sure sign that the value is real. Giving your clients value is the way to build up a solid client base,' I explained. 'What about cost?' I asked Rachel. 'Do you perceive that your repeat clients are less price-sensitive than they used to be?'

'For sure!' she said. 'They almost never question my hours or how much I bill them any more. They know that they are getting value.'

'That's great,' I said. 'So we have repeated sales from our client base and decreased price sensitivity as two indicators of real value. What about new projects?' I added. 'Do you have to pitch for new work or do they come straight to you?'

Now Rachel smiled broadly. 'I don't often compete for work. They know that they will get a great product from me. They have also started referring other divisions to me.'

It was my turn to smile. 'There you have it,' I said. 'The other sure signs that the value is real are when your clients come straight to you, and when they trust you enough to refer others to you.'

'So, I sell customer attraction and my value is real,' said Rachel. 'Suddenly, I'm beginning to feel a bit better.'

I said nothing. I knew that we still had many questions to answer. But, for now, I was content that Rachel was starting to gain a fresh perspective on her business.

Not all entrepreneurs are able to pass the test of 'Is your value real?' About two years before, I had met with a friend's son, Solly, to help him with his new business venture, a stationery shop. I decided that it would be instructive to share Solly's story with Rachel at this point.

'Like you, Solly was struggling with his business and he wanted to give up,' I said. 'I questioned him, in a similar way to what I just did with you, and it turned out that Solly's only real value was price. He tried to attract clients with low prices. But Solly and his competitors were buying from the same suppliers and his competitors simply kept undercutting him. The result was that Solly was unable to retain his clients. It was impossible for him to always be the cheapest. This meant that there was no real value to his clients to consistently buy his goods. All his competitors delivered, they all quoted for jobs, they all promised personal service and, from time to time, Solly was the cheapest so the clients would buy from him. That is no way to build a business,' I concluded emphatically.

'What did you advise Solly to do?' Rachel asked me.

'I applied the "Is your value real?" test,' I said. 'He had few repeat clients, he competed on price, was in endless competition and got no referrals. I advised him to either consider changing his business model or to close the business.'

Rachel and Steve looked at each other. Perhaps, for the first time that day, it was beginning to dawn on them that Rachel would, at the end of it all, have to make a very serious decision. I also hoped that Solly's story would serve another function. I am not a naive optimist. Despite my great love for and support of entrepreneurs, there are times when giving up is the right option. Only time would tell what Rachel should do. The day was just beginning …

The easiest way for small businesses to compete is to offer cheaper prices and personal service. Neither of these lends itself to a sustainable differentiation strategy. There will always be someone cheaper. If you are continually trying to undercut the prices of other competitors, your profit margin will be ever-decreasing and, eventually, the business will not be worthwhile. You will be putting in too much effort for too little reward. While personal service may be attractive, there are only 24 hours in a day. If personal service is your differentiator, this will inevitably limit the number of clients you can service. The value that your company provides has to rest elsewhere. Ideally, the value should reside in an innovative and protectable product or service that allows for the generation of high profits and a long-term relationship with your clients. That is the key to success.

Creating products

'Once you understand the value you are selling, and you know that the value is real, you need to find a way to encapsulate that value into a product,' I said.

Steve had been quiet during my investigation of Rachel's business. He seemed deep in thought.

'There's a problem,' he said, suddenly, 'Rachel is not selling a product. She's selling a service.'

Rachel beamed at Steve's rebuttal. She seemed proud that he appeared to have found a flaw in my logic. The entrepreneur's resistance to turning their passion into a product is something I had encountered before. I had anticipated the question and was ready to show Steve that even those entrepreneurs who offer a service have an obligation to translate their services into products. It is the key to the growth of every small business.

'May I see your wallet?' I asked him.

Both he and Rachel looked at me expectantly. They knew by now that I had another trick up my sleeve.

Steve took out his wallet and I asked him if he had any 'plastic' in it.

'Of course,' he said, handing me a credit card, a petrol card and a store loyalty card.

I held up the gold credit card that Steve had as a result of his bank's deeming him worthy of the 'product'.

'Is your bank in the business of financial service?' I asked him.

'Of course,' came his instant reply.

'And yet,' I said, 'they've found a way to translate that service into the very product I'm holding in my hand.'

'You see,' I continued, 'some of your bank's customers have silver credit cards while others, like you, have gold, and the even more privileged have platinum cards. Each group of clients, represented by the type of credit card issued to them, gets a different set of services from the bank. The bank has simply encapsulated their services in products that they are able to offer to their customers.'

Rachel and Steve sat back in their chairs. It had been a long session and we all needed a break.

I needed to pop out to the shop, as well as dash home quickly, to get some items for a little demonstration I wanted to do for Rachel and Steve, so I suggested that they make some coffee, and told them that I would be back shortly.

The little plastic card that most of us carry in our wallets represents multiple services offered by your bank, packaged into a product, such as a gold card. A leading South African bank offers its gold card clients 'Free comprehensive global travel insurance, automatic debt protection and higher credit limits'. In addition, they claim that these services, as symbolised by the card, represent an annual saving of R8 528.00 for the chosen clients. This piece of plastic is the way in which the bank 'packages' its services. The package allows the bank to target its products to specific markets, thereby enabling the bank to use the product to charge its different clients varying rates.

In the same way that the banks have translated their services into products, so too must entrepreneurs – irrespective of their 'industry' or their 'passion' – find a way to take a defined, tangible product to market.

Cole's Law

Given the insanity of traffic in Johannesburg, I am blessed to live near my offices. I had quickly popped home, and then gone to a supermarket just down the road to pick up supplies, as well as to buy lunch. I returned just as Steve and Rachel were finishing their coffee. I had also brought two chopping boards, two sharp knives, two graters and some bowls and forks into the room. I gave the packets containing the lunch I had bought to my assistant, telling her that we had work to do before we ate. Rachel poured me a cup of coffee as I emptied the remaining contents of my shopping bag onto the boardroom table. I had bought a packet of carrots, a cabbage and a small jar of mayonnaise. I had two additional items, which I left in the supermarket bag, one of which I had brought from home. I left these items in the bags. I would reveal them later, when the time was right. I used to perform magic tricks in high school and I knew that surprise was important in any good show. And I was certainly about to put on a show!

We had settled back around the table and I sensed that it was time to take the discussion to the next level.

'This looks interesting,' said Steve.

'It is,' I said. 'It all started with a guy called Darryl Wolfaardt. He was one of our excellent mentors (or guides as we prefer to call them) at Raizcorp. Unfortunately, Darryl emigrated a few years ago. Before he left, he came up with a wonderful way to help entrepreneurs understand the necessity of creating products, even if they were in a service-based industry. Today's demonstration, in his honour, is called Cole's Law,' I added. I stood up and wrote 'Cole's Law' on the whiteboard. I noticed that Rachel did the same in her notebook.

I handed Rachel one of the graters and asked her if she would please oblige by grating some cabbage. While Rachel began grating, Steve peeled the carrots and I grated them with the second grater. Once we had the required quantity of carrots and cabbage, I put them in a bowl and mixed them together.

I asked Steve to complete the salad by adding some mayonnaise to the grated vegetables.

I then took out the slip that I had brought from the supermarket. I asked Rachel to tell me how much the carrots, cabbage and mayonnaise had cost me. I wrote the three amounts on the whiteboard. I had brought fresh, unpackaged ingredients and so the cost, even with rising food prices, was not expensive at all.

Rachel looked at the completed salad, and looked at the board. 'Oh that's brilliant!' she said. 'Cole's Law is coleslaw.' She and Steve both laughed at the obvious pun.

Cole's Law is coleslaw

Next, with the flourish of a magician pulling a rabbit out of a hat, I reached into the supermarket packet and brought out a tub of ready-made coleslaw.

'Look at that price,' I said, revealing that the tub cost nearly *five times* what it had cost us to make the coleslaw ourselves. Even if you add labour, and the cost of the tub, it was obvious that someone was making a massive profit on what is essentially half a cabbage, two carrots and a bit of mayonnaise.

'What this means,' I explained to my, by now, captive audience, 'is that, if I wanted to take this coleslaw to market, I could sell it at a huge profit. The supermarket has taken three very simple ingredients, combined them, packaged them, named it and, hey presto, you have a product!'

I paused to let Rachel and Steve take in this information. I had just demonstrated what Darryl called 'Cole's Law'. Cole's Law states that it is the entrepreneur's task to combine ingredients (i.e. inputs), add value, find a name, and package a product. Thereafter, the product is taken to market, where, hopefully, it stands out from the other products it is competing with.

I picked up a marker and wrote the very simple formula on the whiteboard:

$$Ingredients + Value + Packaging + Name = Product\ or\ Service$$

'When you, as the entrepreneur, sell that product at a mark-up, you begin to make profit,' I said emphatically. 'You need to decide what a reasonable mark-up is for your product or service in your particular industry,' I added.

Rachel and Steve had obviously enjoyed the demonstration and were now looking quite upbeat. Rachel had also written the formula in her notebook. I offered them each a fork and asked them to taste both the coleslaw we had just made and the coleslaw from the supermarket. I too tasted both of them. We all agreed that there was no real difference between the two and that, in fact, there is nothing very special about coleslaw. It's just a convenient, easy-to-make-or-buy salad.

Cole's Law is essentially about creating a product – what is called 'productisation'. Humans consume more easily those things that they are able to comprehend. When we buy washing powder, we do not buy 'builders, bleach and enzymes', we buy 'Skip' or 'Surf'. And we buy it in identifiable quantities. The entrepreneur's client also wants to buy a product or service that is named, packaged, quantified, and priced correctly. As an entrepreneur, therefore, your challenge is to cater to this desire.

Think of your product in the same way that cellular networks think of their main product, i.e. airtime. Airtime is essentially an intangible service. By packaging airtime into different products, consumers can choose a product which suits their needs and budget. Different products can be bought through a contract or simply as a 'pay as you go' product, where it is available for as little as R5 at a garage shop. This is the essence of productisation.

As an entrepreneur, you need to ask what the equivalent of airtime is in your business, whether it be a product or a service, and find a way to take it, in a tangible form, to your clients.

Specialist lens

I asked Rachel to please hand me her portfolio of work which had been lying unobtrusively on the corner of the boardroom table. Beginning at the back, where Rachel's work for her most recent clients was presented, I noticed that she had designed an advert for a pet shop, as well as a brochure for a pharmaceutical company. This gave me a clue as to where an opportunity for specialisation may lie. I continued to page through for more evidence to support my hunch.

'A lot of your clients seem to be in retail or retail-related businesses,' I commented to Rachel.

'Yup,' she said, 'you're right.'

When working with entrepreneurs, I like to look for trends in their business. I call this my 'specialisation lens'. It was obvious that either on purpose or by accident, Rachel had many retail clients. My specialist lens was suggesting that Rachel was probably a retail-design specialist.

'Why do you think so many of your clients are in retail?' I asked her.

Rachel thought for a few seconds, seemingly unsure of the answer.

'My very first job as a designer was in retail,' she began. 'In fact, even while I was at school, my Saturday jobs were always in the retail world,' she said, seeing the trend for the first time. 'And, when I started Divine Designs, I guess I just continued attracting retail clients. I have contacts in that world and I really understand it,' she said.

'What do you like about the retail industry?' I asked her.

'There's something about the speed of the industry that really excites me,' she said. She now had a big smile on her face. 'Things move fast in retail and you constantly need to be responding to the clients' needs and also predicting what they want. I also love the psychology of why people buy one product over another. I love the buzz!'

She paused for a while before looking up. 'If I think of it properly, my clients are actually not all retailers. Some are retailers and some sell their products through retailers. Does that make a difference?' she asked.

'It may,' I responded, 'but, for now, I am confident that both your retail clients as well as those who distribute through retail are conceptually close enough to each other to fall into a speciality. After all, they're both focused on attracting the consumer!'

I made a circle with my hand and lifted it to my eye. Like a child playing at being a pirate, I pretended to look through a telescope, before saying, 'Through my specialist lens, Rachel, you are a retail-design specialist!'

Rachel grinned. 'I am!' she said, writing the words in her notebook.

'I like the sound of that,' said Steve. 'My wife – the retail-design specialist; it sounds so much more professional than my wife – the designer!'

'It's not more professional,' I explained, 'it's just more specialised, allowing Rachel to begin to look at productisation and then, of course, to find a way to differentiate her products or service.'

Secret sauce

I had one more trick up my sleeve. I reached into my laptop bag and took out the second jar that I had brought from home.

'And specialisation is why I have brought Grandma Sophie's Secret Sauce to help us!' I said, removing the jar from my bag. I was now relishing the opportunity to revert to my magician's role.

Knowing that I now had Rachel and Steve's full attention, I began my tale. 'When my grandmother, Sophie, arrived in South Africa from Poland, just before World War II, she brought a leather-bound book in which she had written recipes learnt from her mother. One such recipe was for the most delicious mayonnaise you have ever tasted. Grandma Sophie was insistent that the recipe was a family secret and she revealed it only to the women in our family. When I got married, my mother revealed it to my wife and, today, I am proud to be able to use it to help entrepreneurs build their businesses.'

'What are you talking about?' asked Steve. 'How does mayonnaise relate to Rachel's business?'

Without answering, I opened the jar and spooned a carefully measured spoonful into the bowl containing the coleslaw we had just made. I stirred the salad and presented it to the bemused Steve and Rachel.

'Taste it,' I said.

'It's delicious,' Rachel admitted. 'Much yummier than the first coleslaw we made and definitely better than the store-bought product.'

'Grandma Sophie's sauce is really just a basic homemade mayonnaise with some unusual spices added,' I explained. 'It's the spices that differentiate this from any other coleslaw you will ever taste,' I added.

I looked directly into Rachel's eyes. 'We have established that you are a retail-design specialist. What you need to do now is work out what your products are and find a way to differentiate yourself in the marketplace. It's simpler than you think because you are already doing it for clients. You're just not doing it with Cole's Law in mind. You need to be taking yourself to market with your equivalent of Grandma Sophie's Secret Sauce so that your business has a competitive edge that is hard to copy.'

'I think that's easier said than done in a service-based business,' said Rachel. 'How in heaven's name do you create a secret sauce in a design agency?' she asked.

Many entrepreneurs who offer a service often baulk at the possibility of having a secret sauce in their business. I understood Rachel's reluctance but was not willing to let her get away from, at the very least, beginning to think about the concept of secret sauce in her business.

'Remember that "secret sauce" is not literally a sauce,' I began. 'One of my favourite sayings is "where there's mystery, there's margin"', I said.

'I like that,' said Steve. 'How does it relate to Rachel?' he asked.

I answered Steve but looked at Rachel.

'Your clients want you to do things that will get people to buy their products. You need to apply your mind to the psychology of buying. Why do people buy things? As you get better and better at it, you will start to put systems and processes together in unique ways that will give you a competitive edge. Secret sauce is simply unrevealed methodology.'

'So, basically, Rachel needs to create mystery around how she works,' said Steve.

'No problem!' said Rachel. I detected a hint of sarcasm in her voice.

'It's not an overnight thing,' I said. 'At Raizcorp, after ten years, we are still working on our secret sauce. What we've realised is that we have various secret sauces in different places in the business. For example, all our entrepreneurs undergo a psychological assessment. We don't reveal to anyone, except the test markers, exactly what combination of qualities we are looking for. Selection is one of the things that makes us a leader in our field. Having a secret sauce in our selection process keeps our competitors on their toes!'

I turned directly to Rachel now. 'Just keep getting better and better at what you do and you will slowly start to work out what your secret sauce is. Don't rush the process. It will come to you,' I said.

Rachel's acceptance that she was in the business of retail design and, more than that, she was a retail-design specialist, was a vital step for her in rekindling her passion for her business. Creating a secret sauce, while important, was not something she needed to worry about yet. The road ahead would still be long and rocky, but I felt that we had made a good start.

In the meantime, the talk of food and sauces had made us hungry and it was, indeed, lunchtime. I sent my assistant a text message to ask her to please bring the lunch into the boardroom.

A local radio station had earlier contacted my assistant to arrange an interview for their business show, which was spotlighting the role of small businesses in the economy. The show's producer had asked me to contact her when I had a ten minute gap. Now was as good a time as any. Excusing myself, I left Rachel and Steve to begin lunch in peace. I felt sure they had much to talk about.

After lunch, we would, metaphorically speaking, be going fishing!

Essentially in a service business, there are two ways to differentiate: specialisation and secret sauce.

You would not go to a GP for heart surgery; on the other hand, you would not go to a heart surgeon for flu. The difference between the GP and the heart surgeon is specialisation. The doctor who becomes a heart surgeon offers a specialist service, is able to charge more and will attract only those clients in need of his or her particular services. The heart surgeon's differentiation is specialist knowledge. Entrepreneurs need to adopt the same approach.

When you specialise you become not only less price-sensitive (i.e. you can charge more with little effect on demand), you are able to attract the clients you want, who know that buying from you is the equivalent of going to the heart surgeon for specialist surgery. In order to apply the 'specialist lens' to your business, you need to look back at your clients. Often, by the nature of how entrepreneurs procure their business, we begin to specialise inadvertently: one client refers another, or you simply begin to seek out clients in similar industries. Before you know it you are, in fact, becoming a specialist. The challenge lies in turning your speciality into a product or, even better, several products that you can take to market.

The second way to differentiate is demonstrated in the difference between the basic coleslaw that you make at home and the 'special' coleslaw with its added secret ingredients. This is because the sauce is literally secret. Many great brands pride themselves on their secret ingredients: KFC and Coca-Cola are good examples of this. But 'secret sauce' is, of course, not literally a sauce. No matter what your business, you need to create your own secret sauce, with a hidden ingredient, which differentiates you from your competition and keeps your customers coming back for more. It is difficult, but the rewards will be worth it.

But are there fish?

I returned from my interview with the producer of the news programme. Rachel and Steve were tucking into lunch. As I helped myself, Rachel asked me how the interview had gone. I responded positively telling her that the producer had wanted my opinion on a recently passed law that would affect small businesses. They would be using a sentence or two as a sound bite on their news bulletin during the week.

'I'm so jealous!' said Rachel. 'I wish I could get media attention without having to pay for it.'

I assured Rachel that this was something we would talk about in due course but that she would have to be patient. For now, it was time to turn our attention to a more pressing matter – her clients.

Allon: So, Rachel, how many clients do you have?

Rachel: About 30.

Allon: And tell me, of these 30, how many have used your services in the past six months?

Rachel: Probably six.

At this point, I began to get annoyed with Rachel. 'You remind me of a teenage boy boasting about his conquests, and including even the girl who gave him a smile,' I said to her. Rachel looked at me sheepishly. She could see that I was not going to buy her delusions of grandeur. 'As far as I'm concerned,' I continued, 'you have six clients and 24 who have used your services in the past. But let's not kid ourselves. You have only six clients. Today is about honesty, Rachel. Finding ways to build a business that has 30 clients is very different from building one that has six clients. Just like the teenage boy, many entrepreneurs also bullshit themselves about just how many clients they have. And then they begin to believe their own bullshit!'

Rachel was visibly taken aback by my bluntness. But I knew that, without real honesty, Rachel would not be able to make the right decision regarding whether to continue running her business.

I looked directly into Rachel's eyes. 'You're talking to me,' I said. 'I'm not looking for information for a marketing brochure!' I added somewhat sarcastically, but it was important to me that we continue in a spirit of honesty and truth. Nothing else would do for a decision as important as the one Rachel needed to make.

'I get it,' she said quietly. 'It's hard for me to admit that, after three years, I only really have six clients.'

I could see tears beginning to well up and hoped that I had not gone too far to make my point.

'How many of these six clients would you classify as retail-design clients?' I asked, knowing that we would now have to focus on the positive fact that Rachel actually had six clients. I work with entrepreneurs who wish they had six clients.

Rachel took a second to consider this before replying that she would consider four of the six to be retail-design clients.

'That's about 65 per cent,' I replied quickly, doing the maths in my head. 'I'm happy with that. We can honestly say that the majority of your existing clients are in retail. And we don't need research to tell us that there is a huge potential market of retailers available to you. At least we know that you're fishing in a lake that has fish in it,' I added. 'Even the best fishing rod in the world won't help if you're fishing in a lake with no fish, but you're fishing in a lake full of fish.'

'I'm clearly not a very good fisherman,' said Rachel.

'No,' I said quickly. 'What you need to do is design a product for this well-stocked lake. You're very lucky,' I said. 'You have a defined and obvious market. What we will do later is work on your bait. But the first step is to determine where the fish are.'

I paused to allow Rachel to bask in the good news before beginning the story of Georgina, an entrepreneur who, unlike Rachel, began a business for a 'lake' that turned out to be devoid of fish.

'As you know,' I began, 'many entrepreneurs cross Raizcorp's door looking for support and guidance. A few years ago I was approached by Georgina, a professional who had recently given birth to a baby girl. Her daughter had severe colic and, by the time Georgina came to see me, the strain of motherhood was beginning to show. She was visibly exhausted and her maternity leave was coming to an end. She had just negotiated with her company to return to work on a mornings-only basis at the office, as she was able to do most of her work from home. In her sleepless nights and long days, Georgina had dreamt of a place where she could leave her baby while she rested, relaxed and even got pampered. She discussed the idea with her husband, who is a lawyer, and, spurred on by Georgina's enthusiasm, they decided to invest their savings in Momma's Place. Based on a business Georgina had seen in the US, Momma's Place would be a spa with a supervised play area for children, staffed by nannies who would look after babies. It would be a high-end place in the northern suburbs of Johannesburg where mothers could relax, have nail treatments and massages, and even sleep if that was what they needed, secure in the knowledge that their children were cared for and safe.'

'It sounds like a great business,' said Steve, who had been quiet for a while.

'That's what Georgina and her husband thought too,' I said, continuing my story.

'Georgina told her family and friends about the idea and they were all very encouraging. Many of her friends were also young mothers and they assured her that Momma's Place was just the kind of place they needed. That, and a bit of internet surfing, constituted Georgina's market research. On the basis of her research, mainly of overseas establishments, Georgina convinced herself that she had hit on a sure-fire business idea. She began to dream of franchises even before Momma's Place opened. She found the perfect spot, in an upmarket Johannesburg suburb, convinced that the area was filled with mothers who would flock to her establishment. Georgina held a big launch and, for about a week, the place was filled with friends, family and curious mothers, eager to enjoy the pampering.'

'So far, so good,' said Rachel. 'What happened?'

'Well, here is where it gets interesting,' I continued. 'After the first week, Momma's Place was virtually deserted.'

'Was it not nice?' Steve asked.

'On the contrary; it was beautiful. But, think about it,' I said. 'What is one of the main differences between the US and South Africa in terms of childcare?' I asked.

Rachel and Steve looked at each other. They were parents and I hoped they would spot the obvious flaw in Georgina's business model.

'I suppose that in South Africa most mothers, especially in the northern suburbs of Joburg, can afford to employ nannies,' said Rachel.

'Exactly,' I replied. 'In the US, where such establishments may do well, the majority of middle-class mothers cannot afford full-time domestic help. The South African reality, whether we like it or not, is that even lower-middle-class people can afford full-time nannies. Momma's Place was a good idea in theory but even though the mothers who Georgina had hoped would frequent her business liked the idea of Momma's Place, it was a novelty that they only really needed in exceptional circumstances, when their nanny was unavailable. The market was simply too small to be dependable enough for a sustainable business. Georgina soon found herself looking towards other markets such as book clubs and bridge clubs. But even those were not big enough to sustain the overheads she was incurring. The bottom line is that, without a market, even the best business idea will not succeed. The product may look appealing, friends and family may support it, but unless you have people willing to buy from you on a regular basis, you do not have a worthwhile business.'

Market research and bullshit market research

Steve and Rachel were now sitting up straight in their chairs and I knew I had their attention. I proceeded to tell them that I had learnt the same lesson as Georgina when I opened my first business, The New York Sausage Factory. Like Georgina, I was encouraged by friends and family. I also set up a stall on the side of the road in Pinetown, a working class area in Durban. From my stall, I offered free sausages, as part of my market research, to passers-by. Of course, when they were free everyone loved them! And so, based on the number of people who took up my offer of free sausages, I decided that this would be an ideal place to set up my first store. Because I saw so many people buying from a KFC outlet on the same street, I was convinced that people would definitely be able to afford my hot dogs.

'What happened?' asked Rachel.

'I opened the store to great fanfare. But, as in Georgina's case, people simply did not come. They walked past my store, heading straight for KFC. You see, because there were a lot of people passing by, it looked like I had a market. But what I didn't know, and what I neglected to check, was that the passers-by were not hot-dog-eaters. Hot dogs were simply not part of their lifestyle. They had not grown up with hot dogs and did not see hot dogs as 'food'. For them, hot dogs were something one served at a children's party – they were not something one ate as a meal in the middle of a working day.'

I went on to tell Rachel and Steve how I had done what I believed to be market research. I had offered free samples, asked friends for advice and compared myself with the established fast food brands. I call this 'bullshit' market research. We ask the wrong people the wrong questions and we look for answers in places that will confirm our theories.

'But I thought you made a success of that business?' asked Steve.

'I did,' I replied, 'but only when I relocated to a mall.

The mall was filled with parents and children, and the business thrived. It only succeeded when I took it to a place where people wanted to buy what I was offering.'

I paused before jumping straight in to the question that most needed asking right then. 'So, Rachel, are you sure there is a market for your product?'

Rachel did not hesitate before responding. 'There is definitely a market. I just don't have a product,' she said.

'Don't worry,' I said. 'We'll have lots of time to work on that. First things first. You are a retail-design specialist and there is no shortage of retail stores. We will tailor-make a product. But there is no point in working on a product until you are sure the market is real.'

Once again, it had been a long session and it was time to take a quick comfort break. I hoped Rachel was beginning to see the light at the end of the tunnel.

Entrepreneurs, despite their best intentions, are not always honest with themselves or others. You have to be honest about how many clients you have. I like to base this calculation on the number of people who have actually used your services in the past six months. In most small businesses, anyone else is not actually a client. Businesses that renew their contracts with you annually are also included as clients.

When investigating a potential market, you need to make sure that you are interpreting the data correctly.

You need to make sure that the market needs or wants your product. Do not rest on false assumptions and do not misinterpret enthusiasm for demand. It is a very different story when people actually have to fork out the money for something.

Knowing that there is a market for your products is essential for business success. A perceived need is not a market. When you perceive that there may be a need for a product, it is essential that you truly investigate your potential market. Without an economic right to exist, no business can succeed in the long term. Very often, entrepreneurs unintentionally do their research in one market – for example, their friends and family – and then they deliver their product to a different market. Your friends and family's enthusiasm must be tempered by a good dose of reality.

Their good intentions may inadvertently set you up for failure. What you need to do is look at what you think is your potential market and then you should carefully study both your competitors' products, as well as the substitutes for your product (e.g. butter/ margarine or tea/coffee). In the case of Georgina and her spa for moms, nannies were her competitor! The most basic of market research would have revealed this to be the case. It was simply easier and, in the long term, cheaper for the mothers whom Georgina had hoped would be her clients, to leave their babies with a nanny. A perceived market is not a market. When you do your market research, ensure that you are asking the right people the right questions. If you don't, you may have great flies for bait, but the fish may eat worms!

Product pioneers and market pioneers

We returned to the boardroom and, as we sat down, Steve told us that he had been thinking about what I had just said.

'I don't completely buy it,' he began. 'If Steve Jobs had applied your theory, I wouldn't have this thing,' he said, picking up his iPad, which had been lying on the desk in front of him all morning. 'How can you test a market for something that doesn't even exist? There was no real market for tablets when Apple introduced the iPad. In fact, nobody even knew what a tablet was.'

It was a great point. But Steve was not finished yet.

'Jobs was a pioneer. Pioneers don't have markets; they create markets,' he stated emphatically before adding, 'Jobs's lake was certainly not full of fish!'

'You're right,' I said to Steve. 'But you need to distinguish between two types of pioneers. There are market pioneers and there are product pioneers. In my opinion, even though Apple certainly pioneered products, Jobs was more of a market pioneer than a product pioneer.

'Actually, Jobs didn't invent tablet technology,' I continued. Steve Jobs, the late founder of the Apple Corporation, is a business leader whose career I had followed carefully, and so I was able to correct Steve.

'In fact,' I said, quite happy that I could show off my knowledge of computer technology to Steve, who considered himself a bit of a techie, 'the GRiDPAD was the first, real tablet computer that we would recognise as such. And it was released in 1989. Jobs made the tablet user-friendly, fast and sexy. In so doing, he created a market for the tablet, where previously there was none. And if you look carefully, you will see that Apple did not invent the PC, the MP3 player or downloadable music. Jobs's genius lay in his ability to redesign these products and then create a market for them.' 'OK, boys,' said Rachel, who was now beginning to get bored with the technology talk. 'Let's not forget why we're here. What does all this have to do with me?'

'The fact is, Rachel, you have a market. You do not have to create the market. It exists. The problem is that you are not taking a defined, tangible product, which you know they need, to your market. You need to invent the product; the market is waiting!'

Henry Ford, whose name has become synonymous with the invention of cars, did not actually invent the motor car. But when he created the Ford Motor Company in 1903, he said, 'I will build a car for the great multitude.' This is the thinking of a market pioneer. Like Jobs, he took an existing product, for which there was ostensibly no market, and created it. Of course, the existing product had to be modified and made attractive for the market, but Ford or Jobs did not rely on market research to determine whether the market wanted the product or not.

Another great quote attributed to Ford is, 'If I'd asked my customers what they wanted, they'd have said a faster horse.' This epitomises the thinking of market pioneers.

> *Jobs and Ford invented markets by improving existing products. If you are an inventor, make sure that there is a market for your product or be certain that you have the ability to create that market. Otherwise, you may share the same fate as GRiDPAD!*

You have to make a profit

We had digressed slightly and so, to remind Rachel that part of having an economic right to exist lies in your business having a product, a differentiator and a market, I offered the following cautionary advice. 'Once you have these three things in place, your economic right to exist rests, ultimately, on your ability to make a profit. Without real profit, your business will not survive.' This seems such an obvious thing to say. However, many entrepreneurs do not fully understand the concept of profit margin. The result is the demise of their business.

I wrote the following words on the whiteboard:

Product   Mistakes   Complexity

'These are the three types of profit margin you need to make,' I explained. 'Most entrepreneurs focus only on product profit margin. They understand that profit is essentially the total selling price less the sum of the costs to produce the product. Only a few actually include the attributable overheads as part of the cost inputs.'

I saw that Rachel's eyes had glazed over as I finished my sentence and so I quickly wrote the formula on the board:

$$Product\ Profit = Sales - \{Cost\ of\ Sales + Attributable\ Overheads\}$$

I suggested that Rachel write down the formula in her notebook.

Calculating your real profit – honestly

As she wrote, Steve said, 'That's not what I learnt in accountancy at school.'

'You're right,' I said, 'and Colin, my partner, who is an accountant, squirms at the way I calculate profit. But this is the most pragmatic way to cost your product or service so that you are able to set a realistic and profitable selling price. If your selling price is too low because you do not understand your real costs, you will end up selling your goods for little or no profit. And, in many instances, you will be operating at a loss without even knowing it.'

Steve did not look convinced, so I continued.

'As entrepreneurs, unfortunately we love to compete on price and boast to our clients that, because of our low overheads, we are able to provide cheaper prices than our larger competitors. If we knew what our real costs were, however, we would not be so quick to offer such competitive prices. The truth is that small businesses have the bad habit of not recovering their overheads. They only look at their direct input costs and are happy when they can recover these at a slight margin. The margin is, unfortunately, usually less than they calculated and seldom covers their overheads.'

47

'But don't we deal with overheads under "expenses" in our income statement?' asked Steve.

I had anticipated the question and I was quick to respond. 'Technically, yes, but remember we're talking about product profit and the reality is that, if small businesses do not incorporate their overhead costs upfront, they seldom recoup these costs. Generally, small businesses do not have a range of products over which they can spread and equalise their costs. If you do not recover your overheads by loading the costing with attributable overheads, you will not succeed.'

Rachel held her hand up. 'Just go back to product profit margin please. I need a bit of guidance there before you and Steve sort out who has the better formula.'

Rachel seemed to be engaged and I hoped that, even though we were dealing with complex concepts, she was beginning to appreciate the importance of costing correctly.

I asked her to please give me one of the files that I had requested she bring to this meeting. She reached into her briefcase and handed me a beautifully covered file. I was reminded of how organised and methodical Rachel was. I opened the file and looked at her client invoices.

'I see that you're charging R450 an hour,' I said.

Rachel looked at me and then at Steve. 'I know I need to charge R650,' she said, 'but then I wouldn't get the work.'

'Don't worry about that now. We'll talk about that later,' I said. 'Let's deal with what you *do* charge.'

Looking at the last invoice in her file, I saw that she had charged her client R4 500 for the design of a brochure. I then asked her to pull out her designer's time sheet for the job. I noticed that her designer had spent eighteen and a half hours on the job.

'Can you explain why you charged R4 500 for eighteen and a half hours work?' I asked.

Again, Rachel looked at both of us. Her reply, when it came, was defensive. 'I thought it would take ten hours,' she said, 'so I quoted R4 500. I couldn't charge them more after that.'

'That's all right, Rachel,' I said, trying to calm her down. 'We need to do this exercise for you to appreciate a very important concept that most entrepreneurs don't get. Where else did you spend time on this job?' I asked.

'Well, I had two meetings at the client's offices, where they briefed me on the job. That took about three hours in total.'

'And how far are their offices?' I asked.

'About 45 minutes away,' she said.

'So we can add three hours for meetings and three hours for travel time to the eighteen and a half,' I said. 'That means we're really looking at R4 500 divided by 24½ hours.' I could see Rachel writing the figures in her notebook.

I asked Steve to do the maths on his phone. He whipped out his mobile and did a quick calculation. The look on his face said it all. 'That's R184 an hour,' he proclaimed. 'So you are actually only charging R184 an hour, and not R450!'

Rachel was silent. I didn't want to add to her woes but, unfortunately, we were not yet done.

'What about your fixed monthly overheads?' I asked her. 'What are you paying in rent, electricity, water and salaries?'

'Oh dear, does it get worse?' she asked. 'If I include the salary of my designer, Mark, my costs are about R25 000 a month.'

I knew that Rachel had not included her own salary in this number. Knowing that we would have to get to that later, and not having the heart to freak Rachel out more than I was already doing, I decided not to mention the salary issue right now. Again, I turned to Steve and asked him to divide R25 000 by 320, representing the average productive working hours in a month (160) for both Rachel and her designer.

'Rachel's overheads are R78 an hour,' he said.

'So, subtract R78 from R184,' I said.

Again, he looked up, ashen-faced.

'I don't want to know,' said Rachel.

'It's R106 an hour,' said Steve. 'No wonder you're not making money!'

There was silence in the room. I noticed Rachel write R106 in her notebook, followed by an exclamation mark. Rachel's short-lived optimism had given way to depression. As she reached for a tissue, I knew that this pain was necessary. I also knew that it would not get better immediately.

'Chill, Steve,' I said. 'Most entrepreneurs actually forget to attribute *any* overheads to their costing. But, by the same token, attributing *all* your overheads is also incorrect.'

I turned to Rachel and asked her, 'What percentage of your total capacity is Divine Designs using right now?'

'What do you mean?' she asked.

'Between you and Mark, what percentage of your day are you really busy with actual client work?' I asked.

Rachel thought for a moment before conceding that, if she had to be honest, they probably spent 60 per cent of their time in productive, client-related work.

Going on my belief that 320 hours represented the average number of productive working hours in a month, for both Rachel and her designer combined, I asked Steve to calculate 60 per cent of 320.

The answer was 192. I wrote this on the board.

While a visibly confused Rachel got up to make a cup of coffee, I paged through her file and roughly added up the number of hours that the company had invoiced for in the past month.

They had invoiced for approximately 130 hours, out of a total 320 possible hours. This represented about 40 per cent of their actual capacity.

Given the fact that Rachel had a habit of invoicing for less than the actual work done, her assertion that they were at 60 per cent capacity seemed plausible.

'So, if we say that you and Mark are working at 60 per cent of your total capacity, we can, therefore, only attribute 60 per cent of your overheads to your costs,' I explained.

'Aha!' said Steve. 'That means the sum we did earlier is wrong.'

'Precisely,' I said. 'If you're only working at 60 per cent of your capacity, then we need to allocate only 60 per cent of your overhead (i.e. R15 000, not R25 000) to your product cost. If we then divide R15 000 by 320, we will get to R47, and not the R78 we previously calculated.'

I asked Steve to subtract R47, being the actual attributable overheads, from the R184 we had worked out we were actually charging an hour.

'So Rachel is actually making R137 an hour, not R106 an hour,' he said. Rachel had replaced 'R106' with 'R137' in her notebook.

'It's not a whole lot better,' she grumbled. Her mood was still visibly depressed.

We still had to account for the other two forgotten types of profit: mistakes and complexity.

I gave Rachel a minute or two to absorb the shock that she was working for R137 an hour before breaking it to her that we were not yet done with this particular topic.

In service-based businesses such as Divine Designs, which effectively sell hours, it is much easier to attribute the overheads to the total possible hours available to 'sell'. However, in small businesses, which sell products, you need to amortise (i.e. distribute) the overheads – that are not already attributed in the cost of sales – over a certain quantity of products sold.

You can become very technical in this regard, and attribute different amounts of your overheads to various products. I suggest that you simply calculate the maximum number of units this business could produce and sell in a month, without expanding any part of the infrastructure or overheads. Then, divide your monthly overheads, which are not already attributed in the cost of sales, by this quantity. This result is the amount you have to recover, per product sold, before you make a profit. This is effectively your breakeven volume.

I realise that this is a very controversial way to do costing. Some argue that it artificially inflates the costs and results in non-competitive pricing, ultimately leading to no sales. My view, however, is that, if the business cannot cover its overheads with its existing capacity, then it will never make a profit and will be forced to close its doors. Amortising the non-direct overheads into the costs will ensure that Rachel creates a more robust business model, hopefully forcing her to differentiate and specialise over time.

There are, of course, businesses which trade in commodities such as petrol, rice, sugar and gold. In these businesses, your ability to make a profit margin through increased price is severely limited. Therefore, the way to create a profit margin is through focusing on process efficiencies and reducing input costs.

The mistakes margin (aka the 'Shit Happens Margin')

I drew Rachel's attention back to the whiteboard and pointed to the second word I'd written earlier – 'mistakes'.

'Small businesses make many mistakes,' I began. 'It takes time to learn to run an efficient business so they often hire the wrong people, buy from expensive suppliers and supply slow-paying customers. Small businesses learn at an exponential rate and so they make relatively more mistakes than mature businesses. In my experience, what this means is that – whatever your costs are – you have to add at least 10 per cent to these costs, for the inevitable unforeseen mistakes that will occur. Basically, if my input cost, calculated correctly for a product, is R10, I will view and represent the cost as R11. It is the only way I can ensure that mistakes will not sink my business.'

Rachel clearly had reservations about this. 'I don't buy that,' she said. 'When I hired my first designer, it wasn't a mistake. The fact that, six months later, she was pregnant and unable to focus, does not make it a mistake that I hired her.'

'That's why I prefer to call it the "Shit Happens Margin",' I said, as Rachel and Steve both laughed. 'The bottom line is that shit always happens. But entrepreneurs do not factor the unforeseen "shit" into their costing. You pay a price when your designer quits, or goes on maternity leave, or becomes unfocused. If you do not factor in the "Shit Happens Margin", you run the real risk of being less profitable than you think you are.'

It was a lesson I had learnt the hard way and it is important to me that entrepreneurs always factor in the shit happens margin to their costing.

> I completely acknowledge that the 'Shit Happens Margin' is not part of any accountancy curriculum, and that, technically, when working out your profitability, it appears nowhere. However, the regularity with which small entrepreneurial businesses experience mistakes, mishaps and random events, makes accounting for these events extremely important. Ultimately, these costs are incurred as additional expenses in the income statement. But I believe that, by notionally building this cost into the product cost, we end up charging the client a far more realistic price for our products or services. I believe that 10 per cent is a good rule of thumb, but this may change from industry to industry.

The complexity margin

'And finally we also need to consider complexity,' I said, pointing to the third word I'd written on the whiteboard earlier.

'So I need to make profit, and I need to factor in shit happening,' said Rachel, looking at the board. 'As if that wasn't complex enough, I still have to factor in "complexity"!'

'No one said running a business is easy. In fact, as your business grows, it naturally becomes more and more complex. That is why you have to factor in what I call the "Complexity Margin".'

'What exactly does that mean?' asked Steve.

I proceeded to explain to Steve and Rachel that, at the moment, Rachel had one designer in her business. When she needs to communicate with Mark, she can simply walk into his office and speak to him. Communication is a simple two-way exchange. As her business grows, and she hires a second designer, communication is suddenly tripled. There are now six lines of communication. Add a third new designer to the mix and suddenly there are sixteen lines of communication! Not only that but, at some point, she will need to make a decision about having staff meetings. In order to have staff meetings, she will need a room large enough to accommodate her growing staff.

As the business grows, the meeting room will become too small for all her staff. The staff meetings will now need to be split, adding an additional layer of complexity. Communication will suddenly be something Rachel will have to think about and plan for. At some point, the business may even need to employ someone to handle communications. Costs such as these will be incurred in all growing businesses.

They are generally not costs incurred directly in the production of the product or sales. They fall into a category called support services or 'unproductive costs'.

Suddenly, despite the fact that she has more business coming in, her costings will not have taken into consideration the costs associated with the inadvertent complexity of a growing business.

'I should be so lucky,' said Rachel.

I smiled. I know what it takes to manage a small business that suddenly gets bigger than your wildest dreams and so I asked Rachel a simple question: 'Can you imagine that, when your business grows, at some point you will need a manager to manage your designers?'

'I'd love that,' she said. I hoped that she was beginning to dream bigger and beyond her current malaise.

'The problem,' I said, 'is that your manager will not actually be working full-time in design. She will be managing the other designers. You cannot suddenly go to your client and increase your costs because you hired a manager. It doesn't work that way. You need to be thinking ahead. That is why I add an additional 10 to 15 per cent to all my costings to factor in the complexity margin.

'Growing small businesses that compete on price often fail because they have not factored in the cost of complexity that growth brings. The "big guys" are forced to factor in the costs of what it *really* takes to produce the product. The receptionist, the cleaner and the manager are all part of what it takes to get the product out to market. If you want to grow your business, the indirect support costs will sink your business unless you begin to make provision for them while you are still small.'

I stopped. It had been quite a lecture but I am passionate about getting entrepreneurs to get their costings right. Although my three types of required profit margin and the way I cost are not something you will find in an accountancy textbook, I know that they are practical and they are real. And, most importantly, costing correctly is what makes the difference between survival and failure for small growing businesses.

'So between "shit happens" and "complexity", I need to be notionally adding at least 25 per cent to my costs, which I then mark up to my clients,' said Rachel.

'Yes,' I replied emphatically. 'If the real product cost is R10, you need to add R1 for the shit that will happen and at least R1.50 to factor in complexity. I would use R12.50 as my cost and then begin to mark up.'

I almost anticipated Steve's next comment. 'Using your formula, Rachel will price herself out of the market,' he said.

'No Steve, what this means is that the drive to differentiate herself becomes even more crucial. Small businesses cannot compete on price. It is the road to ruin. The only way to compete is to convince your clients that you are special and that you can add value to them. Compete by being unique; not by being cheap.

Cheap will limit your growth and, ultimately, you will underprice – not overprice – yourself into oblivion.'

Rachel knew what she was selling and, although we had not yet worked out how to package it as a product, I knew that this would not be difficult. I knew also that we would be able to find her differentiator. She had a market and, although she was not yet profitable, with the right product mix, and the addition of a secret sauce, it was clear that Rachel had an economic right to exist. I felt confident that we could continue. We had spent a lot of time discussing financial issues. And while the bottom line is certainly important, there were many other things that still needed consideration. Next we would be looking at Rachel's non-financial resources.

Checklist for Chapter 2	
Do you know what you are selling?	
Have you productised it?	
Can you productise it?	
Do you have a market?	
Do you have a differentiator?	
Could you have a differentiator?	
Do you make a real profit?	
Can you make a real profit?	

CHAPTER 3

Do you have non-financial resources to tap into?

The truth wobble

The previous discussion on finances had been quite harrowing and so, while drinking coffee, we chatted about things not related to the business. As we talked, I noticed that Rachel kept looking at her notebook into which she had scribbled some of the calculations we had earlier done.

Suddenly, she looked up. 'I cannot believe that I'm making even less money than I thought I was,' she said.

Steve put his hand on her arm. 'At least you know now, and you can begin to work with real figures,' he said.

'Or I can just shut up shop,' said Rachel. Clearly the realisation of the actual numbers had hit her hard.

'Maybe I'm just not an entrepreneur,' she said. 'I'm lying to myself and everyone else. A real entrepreneur would know their numbers. Everyone thinks I'm so successful because I have a business and clients and staff. But when I look at what I'm actually making, it's all just a sham!'

I was not concerned by Rachel's outburst. I told her that I believed she was having a truth wobble.

'A what?' asked Steve and so I explained.

'Many entrepreneurs experience the truth wobble,' I began. 'Someone asks you a question, or you mess up with an order and a client confronts you and suddenly, you panic – they're going to find out that you're not capable! You feel the veneer of success begin to crack. In my experience, honest feedback from someone you love, criticism from a client or, as in your case Rachel, being confronted with your financial reality, may bring it on.'

Rachel and Steve were listening intently and so I continued.

'The "truth wobble" is a knee-jerk, panicked response to genuine feedback from your environment. This feedback, be it in the form of a question or a comment, pierces the veneer of confidence that entrepreneurs require to function. Suddenly, the entrepreneur finds himself asking, "Will they find out that my business is actually a house of cards?" Objectively, however, it is just a question, feedback, or a much-needed reality check.'

'So, what do I do with this reality check?' asked Rachel, obviously still rattled.

'There are three ways to respond to the "truth wobble". Some entrepreneurs can't handle the fact that they've been "caught out". They, the ones who I call "free-fallers", freak out and look for someone to blame.

61

They don't take responsibility and most of them don't survive the "truth wobble". Victims to the end, they go down blaming everyone but themselves for their failure. Then you have the "bouncers". Unlike the "free-fallers", they're not defensive. They can take the feedback on the chin. They process it and, even though they may lose some momentum, they quickly bounce back and begin their upward journey to a new place – just a few notches above where they had previously been. But the "comeback" is short-lived and then they slowly revert back to the state they were before they received the feedback.'

'It sounds like bouncers are like dieters – losing weight and gaining it straight back,' said Rachel.

'Precisely,' I said. I continued by explaining that some bouncers are able to maintain their new status quo and are able to slowly grow their upward momentum. Most don't because their change is a fad – just like a diet. They don't do what the third group do. I call them the 'gliders'. The gliders don't take the feedback well at first. They fight, argue and debate. They then spend time processing the information. They often do not accept all that has been presented and may continue to debate the validity of the feedback. Thereafter, they take the feedback very seriously and make structural and concrete changes that ensure that there is no chance of the old pattern re-emerging in the long run. The solutions are their own and are therefore 'owned', resulting in a more sustainable change. Like a glider, they use the downward momentum, and the wind resistance, to be the force that takes them to new heights.

'What do you think I am?' asked Rachel.

'Only time will tell,' I said. 'We are just getting started. It is completely up to you how you respond to my probing and feedback.'

'It feels like the environment you're speaking of is quite hostile – they probe, they question and they criticise,' she said.

'You can choose to see it that way,' I said. 'Alternatively, you can choose to see these people as valuable resources, helping you to better understand yourself, identify your gaps, give you a different perspective and, ultimately, build your business. These people are very valuable resources in growing your business. What you do with the information is up to you.'

I then told Rachel the story of Stan.

Recognising resources

In the late nineties, I was a partner and marketing director in a vehicle-security company. Although the company was growing, it was increasingly cash-strapped and I was facing yet another month end with not enough money to pay salaries. The other partners and I had exhausted all our sources of finance and closure seemed inevitable.

Like Rachel today, I found myself in a dark place, struggling to find the strength to carry on. I was exhausted all the time and the thoughts churning constantly in my head were driving me crazy. Even when I was managing to keep it together, I felt like a fake. I was at my wits' end when I received a surprise phone call from an old family friend. Stan had heard that I was distressed and he invited me to join him for lunch the following day. We met at an Italian restaurant in Durban and, after exchanging pleasantries and catching up briefly on family news, Stan asked me about the business, and how I was coping with the stress.

I told Stan that, although the business's turnover had been growing, we were struggling to maintain a positive cash flow, let alone be profitable. We were, in my opinion, investing far too much in the research and development of our new vehicle tracking system, as well as in building the market share of our gear-lock business. I explained to Stan that our expenses far outweighed our income. We were about to launch our new product but had quite simply run out of financial runway. Although Stan smiled at my metaphor, he could see that I was seriously worried.

As I spoke, he asked me questions. He probed into the inherent value in the business and asked me many questions about the technology we were using, how much money we had actually invested and where I saw the future market of the business. As we spoke, Stan began to get visibly excited about the business. His excitement was confusing, yet infectious. He was not perturbed by the lack of sales or the technical problems, nor did he seem to care about the current cash-flow crisis that was keeping me awake at night. In his view, these issues were merely temporary teething problems and growing pains.

He forced me to stand back and take an objective view of the business as a whole. This allowed me to acknowledge that the potential of the business was as real as I had believed it to be. As Stan got even more excited about the business's potential, we began to explore other options for finding funding. My spirits lifted and I began to hope again.

The lunch with Stan changed my whole perspective on the business. He managed to give me hope, and his belief, not only in me, but also in the potential of the business, cleared the way for me to continue building it with renewed vigour. After lunch, I returned to work feeling excited and energised. I began immediately to follow up on the new investor opportunities that my lunch with Stan had revealed. My confident and exuberant tone seemed to elicit positive responses from the people I contacted. Within a few hours, I had secured meetings with three potential funders.

What I learnt from my meeting with Stan, and the ensuing path of action on which I set off, was that a conversation with one man had the potential to change my perspective entirely. From being down and dejected, I emerged energised and positive. All entrepreneurs have resources around them. Most either don't recognise them or they are too proud to tap into them. I knew that Rachel too had a vast network of people, all of whom she needed to begin considering as resources.

Many entrepreneurs, when asked, will say that access to finance is the biggest obstacle to the growth of their business.

Research often corroborates this finding. I have never believed this. My experience is that, during the start-up phase, access to finance is not as important as having access to support and information. I was excited to find that the SME Survey of 2005 verified my unpopular point of view.

I have long believed that successful entrepreneurs have a strong belief in their ability to muster resources. The words in the previous sentence are carefully chosen. It is not 'ability to muster resources' that is important. Rather, it is 'belief in their ability'. This means that, at the time an opportunity presents itself, the resources do not necessarily need to be in place, just the belief that they can be sourced. If you find a plumbing opportunity, you do not have to be a plumber to take advantage of the opportunity – you just need to believe you can find plumbers.

Unfortunately, not only do many entrepreneurs not possess the self-belief that they can muster the resources, they do not even look around to see what resources are actually available to them. As a result, they are unable to capitalise on, and leverage off, these resources. Entrepreneurs need to find ways to view their world in the vivid colours of resources – partners, family, friends, siblings, mentors – there are many people available to support entrepreneurs. The secret is to recognise these opportunities and to believe that you have the right to lean on them, benefit from them and, hopefully, move from a lonely, alienated place to a place of positive action.

Non-financial support has the ability to cushion entrepreneurs in all the stages of building a business, both in the good times and the bad. When times are good, some entrepreneurs may become over-confident and arrogant. This could easily lead to ego-based decisions and a decline in fortunes. Often it is a brother, sister or spouse's well-chosen remark that has the ability to bring the entrepreneur right back down to earth. By the same token, when times are tough, it is the same individual's shoulders that are strong enough to give the entrepreneur the required lift.

It takes two

I began by asking Rachel what or whom she would consider to be her biggest resource.

She hesitated and I added quickly, 'It's not a trick question. In fact, your biggest resource is in this room,' I said, looking at Steve.

Rachel smiled. 'You're right,' she said. 'I don't really think of Steve as a 'resource' but if Steve was not there for me, both in the good and the hard times, we wouldn't even be having this conversation now. I'd have given up a long time ago.'

I shared with Rachel and Steve that, in Raizcorp's formative years, not only did my wife, Toni, support me, more importantly she never expressed doubt in me or my mission. In a sea of naysayers, she was the one constant believer.

'We are so close to our spouses that it is easy to take them for granted. We often underestimate the role that a supportive life partner plays in the success story of an entrepreneur,' I said.

'Are all spouses supportive?' asked Rachel.

The answer to that question was easy. I have been privy to many spats between feuding couples and know that an unsupportive partner is one of the biggest influences in an entrepreneur's decision to throw in the towel.

'Of course not!' I replied hastily. 'That is why when you do have a supportive spouse, you need to recognise how important they are to your success.'

Looking over at Steve, Rachel had tears in her eyes.

'Please excuse me,' she said as she hastily left the room. I suspected that the recognition of Steve's role, and the quiet, yet constant, support he offered her was a little overwhelming.

Neither of us stopped Rachel from leaving.

I looked over at Steve, who was looking decidedly uncomfortable. 'How are you doing?' I asked him.

'Fine!' he retorted, a little too quickly to be convincing. I looked at him disbelievingly. He sensed that I was not buying his answer.

'Look,' he said, 'I'm no hero. I often get irritated and, between you and me, I sometimes secretly wish that Rachel would just get a job,' he admitted somewhat sheepishly.

'So, why don't you tell her to do that?' I asked him.

Steve smiled, looking at me as if I were out of my mind. 'She's depressed now,' he said, 'but have you seen the way her eyes light up when she talks about the business? That's when I see the woman I met and fell in love with. She's alive and her enthusiasm radiates passionately. But when she gets down, it is harder each time to lift her up. Truthfully, I'm exhausted by the relentless unpredictability of it all.'

He paused briefly, almost surprised by his own outburst before continuing. 'How do we make plans when we never know how much money she can expect to make from month to month or when we never know how busy she's going to be? Last month we had planned a weekend away. We desperately needed to reconnect and so I found a great, reasonably priced spot in the mountains. We found a dog-sitter, checked out the website for activities we were going to do and, at the last minute, Rachel got a call from Woolworths. They needed her to pitch a new concept by Monday. Needless to say, I spent the weekend watching her work!'

I did not respond, sensing that there was more, and that Steve was relishing the opportunity to express some of his frustration for a change. As predicted, he continued.

'I could live with the last-minute-dot-com stuff, which never seems to end, but the inability to plan our finances is really starting to get to me,' he said. 'We never know if Rachel is bringing home a salary and I never know if, indirectly, I'll be contributing to the business or not. Then she stresses out because she can't help me cover any of the bills. It's an emotional roller-coaster ride.'

He sat back. But he had not yet finished venting. 'Even when she's home, she's not home,' he said. 'She's always working. I can see the look in her eyes. I know when she has work on her mind. Lately, it's the only thing she has on her mind.'

He paused briefly. 'Do you think I'm a bad husband?' he asked. Now it was his turn to have tears in his eyes.

'Not at all!' I replied, without hesitation. 'The fact that you continue to support her – despite the roller-coaster ride of running a business – makes her very blessed. Many life partners would not put up with the vagaries of the journey.'

'But I don't blindly support her,' replied Steve. 'If I think she's making a mistake, or if I think a tantrum is out of line, I'll tell her. In fact, we're here today because I suggested that it was time for a frank look at the business. I believe in Rachel, and love being part of watching her make a dream come true. But, if the dream becomes a nightmare, I will be the first person to advise her to end it. That may sound harsh, but support also means being realistic sometimes.'

It is important that entrepreneurs recognise the role played by their spouse or life partner in supporting them on their journey. Significant others are able to be both encouraging and realistic. At the same time, entrepreneurs themselves need to be sensitive to what life with an entrepreneur entails, and the stress that accompanies the journey.

It is an unpredictable trip, with regard to both the cash flow and the workload. Most entrepreneurs are slaves to their clients' needs, and they are often stressed, which affects their moods and their interactions with people. More often than not, it is the spouse who bears the brunt of the stress.

Whether entrepreneurs are at work or not, they are, as Steve pointed out, constantly working. It is hard for entrepreneurs to find the 'off' button. Life with an entrepreneur, certainly in the start-up years, is stressful. It is important for the entrepreneur to recognise, acknowledge and be grateful for the loved ones who stand by them in this phase of building a business.

Look, Ma, no hands!

We heard Rachel's footsteps approaching. As she entered the room, Steve and I gave each other a knowing look. I felt sure that Rachel knew that Steve also needed to give voice to some of his frustrations. Our conversation would remain confidential, however. Both of us knew that, ultimately, the day was about Rachel and it was time to turn our attention back to her.

'Sorry about that,' she said. 'I just needed a breather.'

Steve got up to hug Rachel and I asked her if she was ready to continue. She gave me a look that said, 'Do I really have a choice?' and we both smiled.

'We were discussing a support network,' I reminded Rachel. 'What about your dad?' I asked.

71

I knew that Rachel's mother was no longer alive and, although she was close to her father, Rachel had been the apple of her mother's eye. Her mother's death had affected her badly.

'Funny you should mention my dad,' said Rachel. 'I had dinner with him just last week.'

'Lucky you!' said Steve. 'He's not my favourite person, but we have all made peace with our differences,' he said.

'Tell me about him,' I asked Steve.

'He's a good man, but he's just so old-fashioned!' said Steve. 'In my family we tell it like it is; in Rachel's family they talk about the weather. It drives me nuts!'

I looked over at Rachel. Surprisingly, she was smiling.

'Steve's right,' she said. 'But we don't get to choose our family. His is loud and over-the-top. Mine is polite and restrained. But, you know, when I had dinner with my dad last week, and I began telling him about the difficulties in the business, he surprised me. I didn't want to share with him at first, but he was really supportive. He doesn't normally show emotion so, when I cried, I was surprised at how consoling and loving he was.'

'That would be a first!' said Steve.

Rachel slapped him lightly on his thigh. 'And he completely surprised me!' she said. 'He offered to spend three mornings a week at the office to help me with the books and also to show me how to quote better. He even offered to phone my debtors!'

'What?' said Steve. 'You never told me that! Did you take him up on the offer?'

'I thought about it,' Rachel acknowledged. 'But then I decided to thank him and say no. The fact that he offered was enough for me,' she said.

'There is no question that your dad is a resource,' I said, having been quiet for a while, letting Rachel talk about her father and recognise that her father was an incredible resource for her, in both her personal and her business life. As her father had run his own business for many years, there was no doubt in my mind that Rachel was not fully utilising her father as a resource. However, confiding in him was a good start.

I explained to Rachel that, as entrepreneurs, one of the things we value most is our independence. Even more than most children, I think that entrepreneurs are most proud when they can say, 'Look, Ma, no hands!' Entrepreneurs value autonomy and to admit defeat – or any kind of perceived failure – to our parents, is not something we do easily. But it is my experience that our parents are generally wiser than that. They understand the web of life, and have been through their own trials and tribulations. When recognised as a resource, and called upon to assist, they are usually honoured. They rise to the occasion and are only too happy to help their entrepreneurial child. Of course, this is not always the case, but it is what I have witnessed more often than not.

In a recently published book designed to inspire teenagers to 'make more money than their parents', the authors interviewed 50 young and successful entrepreneurs[1]. Almost every entrepreneur cited parental support as one of the most significant factors contributing to their success.

It is important for entrepreneurs to recognise the level of support that a parent can provide. For many entrepreneurs, the choice of entrepreneurship may initially be seen as a rebellion against their parents. Despite changes in the world of work, there is still pressure to 'get a real job'. As a result, when times are tough, many entrepreneurs will be uncomfortable about seeking support from their parents. In most cases, the belief that our parents will see us a failure is simply not true. When we make ourselves vulnerable, we give our parents the opportunity to respond to our cry for help, as well as to share their own pain. The lessons they have learnt may be the very lessons you need to learn. But, if you do not reach out for help, they will be unable to support you.

A quote often attributed to Mark Twain seems apposite here: 'When I was a boy of 14, my father was so ignorant I could hardly stand to have the old man around. But when I got to be 21, I was astonished at how much the old man had learned in seven years.'

Do not let fear get in the way of reaching out. Your parents may surprise you!

Don't expect answers!

'What other non-financial resources do you have available to you?' I asked Rachel.

Looking straight at me, she said, 'You! You're my mentor. The first time I heard you speak at a conference, I knew I wanted you to mentor me. I didn't hesitate to ask you.'

'I remember it well,' I said. 'There was something special about you. I agreed almost immediately. I'm not sure you realised then quite how tough it was going to be,' I added.

'She complained endlessly,' said Steve. 'She said you didn't understand her and wondered why she was putting herself through the "torture", as she called it. And yet she continued to make the appointments to see you.'

'It's a little like having a personal trainer at gym,' said Rachel. 'The pain is sometimes unbearable but, in the long run, the results make it worth it.'

'That's a good analogy in terms of the immediate pain and the long-term benefits,' I said. 'But that's about where the comparison ends. You see, unlike a personal trainer, a good mentor or guide doesn't tell you what to do. And you really fought with me, in the beginning, because all I did was ask questions, when all you wanted were answers.'

'I hated you!' she said. 'I recall the one day when I really lost it and begged you to just tell me what to do.'

'I'll never forget that,' I said. 'Do you remember what I said to you?'

'Sure,' said Rachel, smiling. 'You said that I needed to build my fitness levels myself. My journey as an entrepreneur would be filled with challenges and that I needed to learn to find my own answers.'

'Exactly,' I said. 'Entrepreneurs look towards a mentor to give them advice. But that's not a mentor's role; that's an advisor's role. And the problem with advisors is that the entrepreneur becomes too dependent on them. That's why I asked you to think of me as your 'guide', rather than your mentor. A guide allows you to find your own way by asking the right questions.'

'The penny dropped for me in our third meeting,' said Rachel. 'I came home and could not sleep. You had asked me the two questions that changed my life: what makes you special? And why should I buy from you?'

'When I told you that I was creative and I gave personal service, you told me to stop bullshitting. When you told me that that was exactly what you hear from every other design company, I finally understood! It was a huge moment. I'd been fooling myself and it was time to face up to reality.'

Being vulnerable

'So, what about you?' asked Steve. 'Who do you go to when you need a sounding board?'

I told Rachel and Steve that I, too, have a mentor.

'Does he give you as hard a time as you give me?' asked Rachel.

'Where do you think I learnt to be such a tough guide?' I replied, grinning. 'I went to see him a few years ago when my business was growing and I was having problems dealing with the growth. I spent about half an hour telling him how great everything was and about all the deals I was about to sign, and the media exposure the business was getting. He allowed me to talk, and said very little. When I had finished my monologue, he nodded his head and, after about ten seconds of silence, he looked at me and said, "You have one hour with me, Allon, and you've just spent 30 minutes telling me how great you are. Do you want to continue boasting or do you actually want to get some value out of this meeting?"'

'Wow!' said Steve. 'That's quite harsh.'

'Exactly,' I said. 'And I learnt a very valuable lesson that day. The value of a good session with a mentor lies in the entrepreneur's willingness to be both true and vulnerable. Sure, the mentor needs to know what's working and what's going right. But a meeting with your mentor is not a brag session. You need to take your problems and your issues to your mentor and your mentor needs to help you work things out for yourself. He can't do that if you're not open and honest.'

'That's exactly what happened when you asked me what makes me special,' said Rachel. 'I had been trying so hard to make you think I was great and you just saw straight through me. I stopped feeling the need to impress you. The "What makes you special?" question forced me to get real. It would have taken me for ever to get there if I had not found you to mentor me,' she admitted.

'You're right,' I said to Rachel. 'It's those "aha" moments that truly make the relationship valuable and worth the effort.'

Brutal truth

'Doesn't hearing that kind of feedback from your mentor demotivate you?' asked Steve.

'That depends on your attitude to what's being said,' I replied.

I went on to share with Rachel and Steve another story about a time when my mentor had also said something to me that took me and my business to a completely new place. I had learnt my first lesson and was no longer bragging to him. So, in a meeting, I shared with him that we were having real issues with financial systems and controls. I asked him if he could 'lend' me his accountant to help us sort the business out. He looked at me and, without hesitation, asked me why I could not do it myself. It was not the answer I was expecting and I immediately responded defensively: 'I'm the marketing director!' And then my mentor uttered the following unforgettable words: 'Well then, change your title and do it yourself.'

'Your mentor sounds even harsher than you!' said Rachel. 'I never thought that was possible,' she said, smiling at me.

'I was so infuriated by his comment!' I said. 'I felt wounded, even betrayed.'

'What did you do?' asked Steve.

'It took me a while, but I got over myself,' I admitted. 'And I did what he told me to do. I did do it myself and, of course, it was the best thing I could ever have done. I got stuck in and sorted out the financial stuff myself. It turned out to be excellent advice because it forced me to understand the financial side of my business, which I had always avoided. I took responsibility for my business and I had my mentor to thank for not letting me take the easy way out.'

Too often, entrepreneurs who come to me seeking a mentor, expect me to be a 'sage' who will dispense the wisdom they need to solve all their problems. They then get bitterly disappointed when we end up having a conversation, rather than the 'private lesson' they were hoping for. I have learnt, over time, that the 'private lesson' model of mentorship is not good for entrepreneurs. Not only does it create dependency, but it also disempowers them.

As illustrated in my relationship with both my own mentor and with Rachel, a good mentor asks tough questions and gives as few answers as possible. It is the tough questions that make the mentor–mentee relationship work, not the easy answers dispensed from sage to pupil. If I could, therefore, break my own rules and offer three pieces of advice to entrepreneurs seeking a mentor, it would be the following.

The first piece of advice is not to expect answers. A good mentor will allow you to build up your own fitness levels and stamina for the race that is the entrepreneurial journey. Doing it for you and giving you the answers is not mentorship.

Secondly, showing off is a waste of time. If the relationship is to be of any value, then you, the entrepreneur, need to be real and to allow yourself to be vulnerable. The more honest and open you are, the more able your mentor will be to ask the hard questions. Being mentored is not a marketing exercise. You do not have to sell yourself to your mentor.

And that leads, naturally, to the third piece of advice. Be willing to hear the brutal truth from your mentor. Entrepreneurs seek out, and even crave, positive feedback. Often, we are reluctant to hear the brutal truth. We interpret the truth as a message that we are failing. But, in the context of a mentoring relationship, it is, as the cliché would have us believe, the truth that will set you free. The truth, as spoken by your mentor, will allow you to take the remedial action necessary to grow your business.

My relationship with my mentor has been one of the hardest of my life but it has also been one of the most rewarding. Seek a mentor, be open to the questions, be honest and, in turn, allow your mentor to be honest with you.

Organisations and associations

'So, we've looked at the main non-financial resources available to entrepreneurs,' I said to Rachel, sensing that the energy was beginning to wane in the room and that we were soon going to have to break for tea. 'But there is another group of resources that, I believe, many entrepreneurs do not take advantage of. There are many organisations that can be of assistance.'

'Of course,' said Rachel. 'In fact, you introduced me to one of them. I joined the Emerging Entrepreneurs' Association (EEA) on your recommendation, and at the EEA I met someone who told me to join the Advertising Industry Association (AIA). I got one of my biggest leads at the EEA and a brilliant contract from someone I met at the AIA.'

'I don't really see the point of all these meetings that Rachel attends,' said Steve. 'Most of the time it sounds to me like a mutual whining session.'

'Sometimes they are,' said Rachel. 'I've attended a couple of breakfast forums where there was far too much whinging for my liking and I stopped attending. But when you find a good networking association, it is definitely worth it.'

'There's no doubt about that,' I said, agreeing with Rachel. 'One of the greatest advantages of belonging to industry-specific organisations is that you get to hear about the trends in your industry. If you know what others are doing, you are able to navigate your own route more carefully. A good networking association can act almost like a GPS for your business,' I added.

'That's true,' said Rachel. 'It was an AIA meeting that made me realise how digital my industry was becoming. After that meeting, I began increasing the portion of revenue I was generating from digital work. Today I would say that it accounts for more than 30 per cent of my income – purely because I saw where the industry was going.'

'That's spot on,' I said. 'It's very easy for entrepreneurs, bogged down by the daily strains of staying afloat, not to see which way the wind's blowing. Being part of these organisations helps you to spot trends.'

'I guess you're right,' said Steve. 'I imagine it also helps you to see what others are doing,' he admitted.

I suspected that Steve would be happier now to let Rachel attend the meetings in future.

Too many entrepreneurs do not take full advantage of the large number of entrepreneurial organisations, industry associations and chambers of commerce available to them. But, in my experience, these are vital to the success of a small business. Not only do they supply a benchmark against which to measure yourself, but they also give you access to the value chain of your industry. They provide great opportunities for learning. I have met both customers and suppliers in the associations with which I have chosen to affiliate. Moreover, the new opportunities that have come my way from networking meetings I have attended have proved invaluable to the growth of my business. I have also made personal friends and, when the going gets tough, these friends have been vital to me. The only warning that I feel compelled to share is that, if you find yourself within a bunch of complainers, get out!

Do not get trapped in the company of negative people. As my friend Kumaran Padayachee says, 'You need to seek out groups attended by winners, not whiners.' Find positive people, those who are in a better situation than you; aspire to learn from them and, hopefully, to emulate them. Be proud to be associated with them.

Checklist for Chapter 3

Do you have the support of a significant other?	
Do you acknowledge this support?	
Do you have the support of a parent/close family member?	
Do you share information with your parent/family?	
Do you ask your parent/family for help?	
Do you have access to a mentor?	
Do you meet your mentor regularly?	
Are you able to be honest and vulnerable with your mentor?	
Do you belong to any entrepreneurial organisations, industry associations or chambers of commerce?	
Do you attend the meetings of the abovementioned groups?	
Do you take advantage of your membership of the abovementioned groups?	
Do the people you associate with have a positive attitude?	

CHAPTER 4

Can you do something else in order to bring in cash?

Your shadow resources

'I definitely feel better knowing that I have a whole lot of people to lean on, and also to ask for help,' said Rachel. 'But none of those people can help me generate cash. And cash is what I need most right now,' she said.

I did not respond immediately. I'd had a feeling that we would get to this topic at some point.

'Give me a second,' I said to Rachel and Steve, as I got up to leave the room. I went quickly to my office and returned with a pack of playing cards.

Both Rachel and Steve looked at me expectantly as I put down the pack of cards on the table. This was not an ordinary pack of playing cards. Displayed prominently on the front of the pack were the words 'Allon Raiz's Entrepreneur's Inspiration Pack'.

'This pack of cards solved my cash-flow problems,' I said to Rachel and Steve.

Addressing Rachel, I said, 'I know your situation. I've been there. A few years ago, when I was in desperate need of cash, I followed a process that taught me invaluable lessons about being an adaptable entrepreneur. I was so desperate that, one day, I just wrote down everything and everybody that I could think of as my resources.'

'Oh no!' said Rachel. 'We're back to resources!'

'Yes, but these are different resources,' I said. 'I call these your "shadow resources". They are all the things you have available to you but that you're not seeing. Or you're seeing them, but not finding ways to utilise them properly to solve a client's pain.'

It was clear to me that Rachel and Steve did not quite understand me. 'Let me tell you how these cards originated,' I said, 'and then you'll know what I'm talking about. As I said, I was desperate for cash and I had sat down and brainstormed every single person and thing that I could think of as a resource. I took a detailed look at my resources – my car, my wife, the office I worked in, the advertising agencies that were Raizcorp's partner businesses, even my knowledge of entrepreneurship and entrepreneurs. I kept on expanding my resources, all the while forcing myself to go beyond the obvious. I just wrote them all down. As I listed them, I began to see just how many resources I had available to me. Eventually, exhausted, I had listed 242 resources. I knew that somewhere, in that list, lay the solution. As I surveyed the list, I began to let my mind wander. I looked at the different resources and began to focus on all my clients and, more importantly, my potential clients – people with whom I had had unsuccessful meetings. One by one, in my mind, I played back the movies of meetings held and rejections experienced. I saw the events unfold, from the pre-meeting anticipation to the post-meeting dejection. I just sat quietly in my office and watched the scenarios, as they had unfolded. I knew that, somewhere, on my list of expanded resources, there was a potential client who had pain that I could fix.'

'That's the second time you've mentioned a client's pain. What do you mean by "pain"?' asked Steve.

Rachel laughed. She had attended my sales courses and she knew that, for me, the secret to a successful sale lay in the ability of the entrepreneur to identify their clients' pain, and then find a way to alleviate that pain for them. I did not need to explain this to Steve. Rachel did it for me.

'It's very simple,' she said. 'Everyone has needs. Entrepreneurs have to see their clients' needs as pain that needs relieving, and then find ways to sell them a solution for their pain.'

'Got it!' said Steve. 'Let's hear what happened with the cards.'

'So, there I was, almost in a meditative state and, in my mind, I happened upon the memory of a meeting I had had with a marketing executive at a large bank. I had approached her to see if she would be interested in sponsoring the launch of Entrepreneurs' Organisation (EO) in South Africa. EO is a highly successful non-profit international entrepreneurs' organisation with over 8 000 members in more than 45 countries. I, and two friends, Orrin Klopper and David Dworcan, wanted to launch a local chapter of EO in South Africa. We needed a sponsor to provide us with seed money to do this. The marketing executive of the bank loved the idea, but, she explained to me, even though she had access to a considerable budget, she needed to reach thousands of people. EO did not, at that point, have a large enough reach for her to justify the spend. Although I understood her position, I walked away from that meeting completely dejected.'

At this point, Rachel and Steve were listening intently and so I continued by telling them that, a few weeks later, when I was playing back the 'movies' of these conversations with my clients, it hit me: there was her pain! She had available budget, but no idea how to reach the thousands of people she was mandated to reach. I looked down at my list and, suddenly, seeing her pain in that light, allowed me to look at my resources anew. I repeated the words to myself 'high reach'. What did I have? I asked myself.

I looked at the list. On it I had written 'knowledge of entrepreneurs and entrepreneurship' as a resource. Until then, I had only shared this knowledge of entrepreneurship with others in a classroom or a mentoring situation. What if I wrote it down?, I thought to myself. What if I dispensed that knowledge in a different way? Then I asked myself what other resources I had listed. At number 28 on my list, I had noted that I had a shareholding in an advertising agency. Until then, I had viewed the agency only as an income generator. As my partner, they shared their profits with Raizcorp. What if I saw them differently? What if I were to be *their* client?

And then, in an instant, I saw the answer. I saw the entrepreneurial knowledge that I possessed written down, concept by concept, tip by tip, on a deck of 52 cards. I saw the deck of cards designed and printed by the advertising agency. And I saw myself solving the marketing executive's pain. A deck of cards – branded with the company's logo – was easily distributed to thousands of people! I picked up a pen and began writing. By the end of the week, I had 52 pieces of entrepreneurial advice and inspiration for entrepreneurs.

'Wow!' said Steve. 'Did she buy it?'

'She did,' I said, smiling, as I opened the pack of cards that I had brought into the room. 'I worked really hard to sort and order the advice. I sorted each suit into a different theme – clubs for networking tips; spades for building block-tools for entrepreneurial businesses; hearts were tips to stay passionate and keep motivated; diamonds contained lateral-thinking exercises. I was so proud of my achievement!'

'I then asked the advertising agency to give me a quote for designing the cards. At first, they were surprised. They were not in the habit of doing work for me, but this job proved to be the first of many successful collaborations. They agreed that I would pay them when I concluded a sale of the cards. With a mock-up in hand, and despite her initial resistance to meet again, I persisted and managed to secure another meeting with the bank's marketing executive. I spent a sleepless night, preparing for the presentation, but my fears proved unfounded. She loved the idea and promised to take the concept to her superiors. True to her word, a week later, she called me to another meeting where we negotiated a price and then, to my utter amazement, we closed the deal with an order for 10 000 packs. We agreed on a 50 per cent deposit and, suddenly, I had cash. Lots of it! I could breathe again.'

Rachel was the first to respond, '10 000 packs!' she exclaimed.

'I couldn't believe it either,' I said. 'It felt like winning the lottery!'

I sat back. It had been a while since I'd told that story. It had truly been a turning point on my entrepreneurial journey.

When entrepreneurs need to generate cash flow, first of all they need to identify a client or a potential client's pain. Next they need to dedicate time to expanding their resources on paper in the most microscopic detail possible. When they have a comprehensive list of resources, they must then find an innovative way to combine these resources to create a product that will allow them to bring in money quickly.

The expansion of resources is very important – you need to be both linear and lateral, i.e. see everything at your disposal as a resource. Your education, for example, is a resource, as is your car. Often, these resources lie in our blind spot. That is why I refer to them as 'shadow resources'. Our shadow is always with us. It is only when we actively turn our attention to it that we actually see it. It is the same with our resources: what are you not seeing?

> *Then, with your client's pain in mind, you need to take a careful look at the resources and find ways to combine them in such a way that you can present your client with a solution.*

Combining resources

'That's very clever,' said Steve. 'The problem is, not all entrepreneurs are as lateral thinking as you,' he added sarcastically.

'Or as rich in resources,' said Rachel quickly.

'It doesn't have to be complicated,' I said. 'I used this process to help an IT company that was cash-strapped and they found an easy solution to bring in cash quickly. At the time, they provided their clients with hardware and software and, as part of their sales process, they would also provide clients with an IT security audit.'

'What do you mean?' asked Rachel.

'When they went into a company, they would check the company's systems and let them know, from an IT perspective, what security systems they needed – for example, firewalls and password security. I helped them to create a template for this process and, rather than offering it for free, they began to sell the audit report for cash. Virtually all their potential clients needed the audit and, by selling the service separately, they not only got regular cash flowing into the business, but were also able to establish relationships with potential clients.'

'How is that the same as what you did with the cards?' asked Steve.

'Well, they weren't seeing their ability to do a quality audit of a company's IT security as a resource; nor were they seeing that all their clients needed it. The simple combination of those two insights allowed them to transform the audit into a stand-alone product, and sell that product. It was an easy sell and it did not distract them from their real intention, which was to sell hardware and software. It really is not a complex process. It just requires a bit of work,' I said.

'I actually get it,' said Rachel. 'I've just realised why Carlos, who owns the fruit and veg shop around the corner from my house, is doing so well! He may not have known it but come to think of it, he did exactly what you're saying.'

Steve and I both looked at Rachel, who had seemingly come back to life again.

'Carlos's shop was really quite a sad place,' she said. 'He took it over from his dad, who had run it as a traditional greengrocery for years. But it was deteriorating. His older customers had moved on and people preferred to go to supermarkets. Now it's totally revamped and pumping again.'

'Are you talking about Carlos who you designed those stickers for?' asked Steve.

'Yes,' replied Rachel. 'Have you not noticed that he sells new products now?'

'No,' said Steve. 'The last time I checked he sold fruit.'

'Typical male,' said Rachel. 'He now has a whole refrigerator full of fresh, ready-prepared fruit and, ever since he started cutting up his fruit and packaging it, his place is full again,' said Rachel.

'And your point?' asked Steve.

I smiled. I had a feeling about where Rachel was going with this. And, if I was correct, it would prove that she had really grasped the point of my earlier stories.

I listened intently as Rachel explained that Carlos had told her that he started preparing and packaging fruit because he kept on hearing his customers either complaining that they didn't have time to peel and cut up fruit, or that they didn't want to buy things that they did not know were ripe and ready for eating.

'He heard his client's pain,' I said.

'He definitely did,' said Rachel. 'At first, I thought it was ridiculous. Who would want to pay 50 per cent more just to save time and see inside a melon? But, on weekends, people are now queuing in his shop. And two of his employees, who used to stand around waiting to find customers a "nice watermelon", are now cutting up fruit. So he is using these resources differently now.'

'He pleases his customers and uses his resources efficiently,' I said. 'What more can a businessman ask for?'

'Amazing,' said Steve. 'I never thought about it like that. But, when I think about the hectic lives that people lead these days, I can see that they don't have time to peel and cut up fruit. Selling ready-prepared fruit really does remedy that pain.'

'Good for Carlos!' I said. 'It sounds like he could teach a lot of entrepreneurs a thing or two. Now it's your turn, Rachel,' I said. It had been a very long day, filled with both information and emotion. It felt like a good time to break.

'What do you mean it's my turn?' asked Rachel.

'I want you to do this exercise,' I said. 'I want you to expand your shadow resources, find your clients' pain, and then I want you to combine your resources to find something to sell your client. You need to find a way to bring in cash and you need to do it quickly.'

Rachel looked at Steve, almost as if she wanted him to come to her rescue.

'Don't look at me!' said Steve. 'You heard the man. You can do it! And at least it's something concrete. You don't have to sit around moping, waiting for the phone to ring or making more cold calls and getting negative responses.'

'Fine!' said Rachel. 'I'll do it.'

And so, on that rather defiant note, we decided that it was time to adjourn for the day. Rachel had homework to do and I hoped that, despite her initial resistance, she would indeed complete the task. It was an important step in her journey towards making the decision to give up or continue to build her business. We agreed that my assistant would contact her to schedule a meeting for three weeks' time.

Oxygen for the business ...

Three weeks later, as arranged, I arrived to find Rachel waiting for me in the Raizcorp boardroom. This time, she was without Steve – but not alone. She had brought Mark, her designer, with her. After the initial introductions and other pleasantries, Rachel explained that she had asked Mark to accompany her, as he had played a pivotal role in the events that had unfolded since last we met. She mentioned, as well, that Steve had offered to bring lunch and would be spending the afternoon with us. Mark indicated that he would need to leave just before lunch, as he had a prior engagement to attend. With these arrangements behind us, and cups of coffee in front of us, I asked Rachel how she had fared with her homework task. She told me that, for a few days after our meeting, she hadn't been able to do anything.

'I was so exhausted I could hardly get out of bed,' she said. 'I was also intimidated by the task,' she admitted. 'On the third day, I finally got out my notebook and I did exactly what you said. I just expanded my resources. I listed everything I could think of. I even listed my dogs as a resource,' she laughed.

'Don't joke,' I said. 'Many people have made a lot of money from seeing others' pets as a resource.' I told them that my dog is groomed monthly by a mobile dog-washing service. Nikita, an ingenious entrepreneur, has a fully equipped bakkie where dogs can be washed, clipped and groomed in the comfort of their own driveway. The business is a perfect example of going beyond the obvious to provide a much-needed professional service that eliminates the need to transport dogs or take them out of their own environments. But we had digressed and so I asked Rachel to continue.

'So I completed the list and during the day I replayed the movies of my clients and my meetings in my head. One meeting kept coming back to me. About two weeks before Steve and I met with you, I had gone to see Lorraine, the marketing manager of SWEAT, a sports retail chain for which I had done some packaging designs. I was hoping she had some more work to pass my way, but on that day she was in a bit of a state. She was late for the meeting because her chief national window designer had just resigned. And, as if that wasn't enough, she was also stressed because she needed to come up with a concept and prizes for the chain's upcoming five-year anniversary promotion. With 78 stores, and no national window designer, the last thing on her mind was packaging and she was quite candid about telling me that. I left the meeting depressed and hardly gave it a second thought until you told me to start looking for my clients' pain and, at the same time, expand my resources.'

'Let me guess,' I said, looking over at Mark. 'You brought one of your resources with you today.'

'Exactly!' she said. 'Here was my designer, sitting at his computer, twiddling his thumbs, waiting for me to bring in the work and I was only seeing him as my designer, nothing else. In expanding my resources, I remembered that Mark had started his career as a set designer for the theatre. I looked at him and I thought to myself, what if, instead of seeing Mark as a graphic designer, I saw him as a set designer? He could help Lorraine to design and dress her shop windows for the upcoming anniversary celebrations.'

'How did you feel about that Mark?' I asked.

'I was quite excited actually when Rachel shared her idea with me,' he said.

'I told Mark about some of the things we had spoken about at our last meeting, and I showed him the list of expanded resources,' said Rachel. 'I told him that, somewhere on that list, was a way for us to make money.'

'We started talking,' said Mark. 'We put clients together and we came up with absurd combinations. We laughed a lot,' he said, smiling at Rachel.

'It's been a while since we've done that,' Rachel responded.

'And then it hit us. We have a client who needed prizes for a birthday promotion. And we have a client who is a tour operator. We had created brochures for special package deals they were offering to Thailand. And we have another client who makes energy bars. I had designed their packaging.'

At this point I was completely intrigued. I pride myself on my ability to combine the oddest of things, but even I was struggling to see the connection. Perhaps they could see the puzzled look on my face as Mark said, 'Don't you get it?'

'Lorraine needed a prize for her promotion. I asked the tour operator if, in exchange for great publicity in 78 stores, they would offer a package holiday to Thailand as a prize. I then asked my customer who makes the energy bars if they would be interested in inserting discount vouchers for a sports shop into their energy bar packaging.

During the promotional month, each client would get a complimentary energy bar and would be informed that they could claim the discount on any purchase made within SWEAT's birthday month. Using the voucher would make the customer eligible for the draw to win the grand prize!'

'Did they all go for it?' I asked.

'They did indeed, with a few tweaks,' said Mark. 'Rachel and I made a formidable team!'

'I hope you asked for a deposit,' I said.

'Of course I did,' said Rachel. 'They only agreed to a 40 per cent deposit and that cash is going to be oxygen for the business,' she added.

Rachel explained that, ordinarily, it would have taken much longer to secure a deal such as this, but the client was under enormous pressure and so her company was awarded the contract relatively quickly. As she spoke, I could not help but notice the difference in tone between Mark and Rachel. Mark's exuberance was palpable, whereas Rachel, although excited, was much more subdued than Mark. I did not say anything, leaving Mark, who tended towards the dramatic at the best of times, to rave on about the deal and to share all his ideas with us.

Glancing at his watch, Mark realised that he needed to leave. Steve had not yet arrived with lunch and I was glad because I knew that this would give me time with Rachel to discuss my perception that she was not quite as excited about the impending project as her designer.

Thanking Mark for joining us, we bade him farewell. For the first time since we had begun meeting, Rachel and I had some time alone. I planned to make constructive use of the time.

Checklist for Chapter 4	
Have you identified a client or a potential client's pain?	
Have you spent dedicated time expanding your resources on paper in the most microscopic detail possible?	
Have you considered your shadow resources (that are lying in your 'blind spot')?	
What are you not seeing?	
Have you found an innovative way to combine these resources to create a product that will allow you to bring in money quickly?	

CHAPTER 5

Do you believe in your abilities?

The competency crisis

Mark had left and Steve had not yet arrived with lunch. I sensed that all was not good with Rachel.

Allon: What's going on?

Rachel: What do you mean?

Allon: It was clear to me that Mark was very excited but you seemed anxious, almost distracted.

Rachel: Nothing's going on.

At this point, I gave Rachel a look, the kind of look that people who know each other well can give each other; the look that says 'don't bullshit me'.

Rachel: Is it that obvious?

I said nothing. A few seconds of silence ensued before Rachel, looking away, said, 'I don't know if I can do it.'

Allon: Do what?

Rachel: My contract with SWEAT is the biggest and most important one I have ever had. I just don't know if I can deliver on it.

Allon: Why?

Rachel did not respond to my question, and was still unable to look at me. I said nothing, knowing that she would, eventually, let me know what was troubling her. At last she spoke, telling me that, after their meeting to make final arrangements and sign the deal, Lorraine, the marketing manager of SWEAT, had uttered the words that were now giving Rachel sleepless nights. Lorraine had asked her, 'Are you sure you can deliver on this project?'

I asked Rachel how she had responded.

'My heart skipped two beats,' said Rachel, 'and I said "absolutely". And, as far as Lorraine was concerned, I meant it. On the outside, I was completely confident; on the inside, I was shaking. By the time I got to my car, I was a bundle of nerves. When I got back to the office, I had convinced myself that we were going to mess this one up. Poor Mark, I was a wreck! He has been at the receiving end of all my anxiety.'

I explained to Rachel that these thoughts were completely natural. She was quite simply going through what I call a 'competency crisis'.

Rachel, of course, wanted to understand exactly what I meant. Just then her cellphone rang. It was Steve calling to say that he had been delayed, and that lunch would be late. So I suggested that Rachel grab a cup of coffee in the meantime.

Steve's call could not have been more opportune. The competency crisis is such a critical, yet normal, milestone on the entrepreneurial journey that I was glad to have the private time to reassure an obviously delicate Rachel that she was not the first entrepreneur to experience these doubts.

'When you started your business, you went out to potential clients and you sold something that really didn't exist yet.'

Rachel nodded. She knew exactly what I was talking about. 'Like all start-up entrepreneurs,' I continued, 'the way you initially portray your business almost never equals reality. The "space" between how you portray the business and the actual reality is like that space when you are dreaming, but are somehow conscious of the fact that it is a dream.'

Rachel smiled. 'I know it is a cliché, but I often feel like a duck, gliding elegantly on the water's surface. Underneath, I'm paddling frantically!'

I could not help smiling. Unfortunately, 'act as if' has to be the mantra of many a start-up entrepreneur.

I asked Rachel if she had ever heard of the 'reality distortion field' and she shook her head. I told her that the term was coined by one of Steve Jobs's colleagues. Jobs had the ability to use his charm and charisma to make people believe that anything was possible. Jobs believed he could deliver and he did. Many people are convinced that Apple's success lies in Jobs's optimism that the impossible was possible.

'The question,' I said to Rachel, 'is whether you believe in your ability to turn your "impossible" into "possible".'

Rachel did not reply. I could see that she was deep in thought and so I continued. 'Holding it together, on the way to success, is a full-time job. It takes energy. The reality for entrepreneurs is that you have to live with the contradiction of presenting what "could be" as the reality. We're not talking about unethical or immoral behaviour. We're talking about "acting as if" in order to succeed. Pretending is not the same as lying. And then the day comes – which is exactly what has happened to you – when the pretending pays off and suddenly you have to deliver!'

I paused to allow Rachel to take in what I was saying before continuing. 'What you need now is to recognise the "competency crisis" you are having and deal with it – there is no going back. This account will take your business to a new place.'

'Competency crisis,' said Rachel. 'I like that – it's a nice way of saying "shit-scared".'

'Fear is definitely a big part of the crisis,' I said, smiling. 'The competency crisis is really about doubt. Doubt in your ability – your ability to deliver, your ability to build a bigger organisation and then your ability to lead that organisation. Not unlike the dog that eventually catches the truck it's been chasing. What does it do with the truck once it's been caught?'

> At the risk of sounding sexist, I have always believed that women's ability to apply make-up gives them a strange advantage over men, in that they are able to use the make-up to portray their features in the best possible way.

They can quite literally put their 'game face' on. Make-up enhances what already exists. Start-up entrepreneurs need to apply 'make-up' to their businesses. This is the basis of 'act as if'. History is filled with entrepreneurs who have pretended to be what they not yet are. The entrepreneur's quality of being able to visualise future scenarios – and to begin acting in a way that is commensurate with these future scenarios – is one of the secrets of success. It is epitomised by entrepreneurs who speak of 'we' when actually they have a one-man business (and 'I' would be more accurate).

Kathy Delaney-Smith was the coach of the Harvard women's basketball team. This description, from a blog by Adam Brotman, so aptly describes the power of the 'act as if' philosophy that I have taken the liberty of quoting it here in full:

> *This is an amazing story of a woman who didn't have experience coaching basketball, but acted as if she could, and went on to lead her team to one of the biggest upsets in NCAA basketball tournament history. She then went on to harness her own 'act as if' philosophy while taking cancer head on. I'll never think about anything else other than this coach and her amazing story when thinking about the power of acting as if. In a* New York Times *article from 2009, Melissa Johnson writes about Delaney-Smith's philosophy: 'Any decent athlete, salesman or Starbucks barista can put on a good game face.*

But her philosophy, "act as if", goes much deeper than mere swagger or theatrics. It's a method — a learned skill for convincing your mind that you already are what you want to become. The body follows where the mind leads."[2]

There are those who disagree with this view. They see 'acting as if' as deception or, even worse, lying. I am not advocating either of these. The unfortunate reality is that it is a gamble to start a business and it is a gamble for others to support a start-up business. At some point, a leap of faith is required.

You need to present your business as having reached a level of success that you know it has the potential to reach. There is no doubt in my mind that when you act as if you are successful, you are more likely to be treated as a successful person. It is a virtuous cycle that breeds success. A word of caution: it all falls apart if you don't have the substance to back it up. Do not say things that you do not mean and do not promise what you cannot deliver.

The bearded phase

'So you're saying that what I'm feeling is perfectly normal?'

'It really is normal,' I said. 'A few years ago, I was working on securing a very big deal – at the time it was worth 36 times our annual turnover. I knew that this was the opportunity that would change everything. I had worked on it for 18 months and, after celebrating the elation of securing it, I was faced with the sobering realisation that we now had to deliver.'

'What did you do?' asked Rachel.

'I grew a beard!' was my reply.

Rachel looked at me as if I was mad.

'My terror at the need to deliver, and the subsequent questions regarding my abilities, distracted me to such an extent that, one Monday morning, I simply forgot to shave. Catching my reflection in the mirror and witnessing the three days' growth, tinged with a bit of grey, I saw somebody else. I bore witness to a different me – a more mature, even older, me. And as I grappled with the questions – Could I deliver? Did I know how? Did I have the leadership skills? Could I muster the resources? – I decided not to shave until I had worked out the answers for myself. And so I went public with my competency crisis. At Raizcorp, this period is now known as my bearded phase. It's an apt metaphor for the crisis because, for most entrepreneurs, the competency crisis precipitates a good dose of growing up.'

'And so,' asked Rachel, 'how long before you shaved?'

'I sported my beard for about two months. It was a difficult time, but I finally worked out that I was indeed the right person to take the organisation to the next level. I knew that this deal was the game-changer and, despite my fears, I knew that, with the right team in place, I could lead Raizcorp to the next level. The deal you have just signed is your game-changer, Rachel.'

Rachel was quiet for a few moments before she asked me, 'But how did you come to that conclusion – how did you know you could lead Raizcorp to the next level?'

'I did exactly what you have done,' I replied. 'I went to my mentor. I wish I had gone to him earlier, when I had more stubble and less of a beard.'

'What did he do?' asked Rachel.

'Don't worry,' I said. 'I'll do it to you.'

> *When starting out, in order to succeed, all entrepreneurs must believe in their ability to deliver. Unfortunately, in the start-up phase, they lack the opportunity to prove it. The veneer of 'I can do it' is necessary to secure the work. For entrepreneurs, this is a very vulnerable time. You need to work hard to maintain the veneer. It is easy to buckle, and even give up, in this phase. 'Acting as if' takes energy. If you don't give up, you will, at some point, begin to secure bigger clients. It is this moment of triumph that may, in all likelihood, precipitate the competency crisis.*
>
> *The competency crisis presents itself when the entrepreneur actually secures the opportunity to do the work, but then loses the belief in his ability to deliver. It is important to remember that this is not about your actual competence. It is about your belief in your own competence, as well as your belief in your ability to muster the resources needed to deliver. The way through the competency crisis, therefore, is to test for these competencies, which we will demonstrate in the next section.*

Do you deserve it?

Turning to Rachel, I said, 'We need to check whether you do indeed have the competencies to deliver on the deal. Let's subject your competency crisis to a reality test.'

'I'm ready,' she replied, although her quick reply belied her growing anxiety. And so we began …

Allon: What changes as a result of your getting this deal?

Rachel: What do you mean?

Allon: Do you need to move premises?

Rachel: No. Our current offices can handle it.

Allon: Do you need more staff?

Rachel: Yes.

Allon: Why?

Rachel: We have a lot of work to do!

Allon: How many people?

Rachel: At least three more part-time designers.

Allon: So you will be going from two employees, Mark and your bookkeeper, to five employees. Have you ever managed that many people before?

Rachel: Sure. In my past jobs, I've managed much bigger teams. I'm not worried about managing them. The only difference is that now I'm responsible for paying them all.

Allon: OK. But you've done your sums. When you quoted, you factored in your costs?

Rachel: Yes, I did.

Allon: And your complexity margin?

Rachel: I resisted at first, but, yes, I did all my sums. I even added in the 'shit happens' margin!

And so Rachel and I continued testing each of her fears, one by one. I attempted to show her that, essentially, she was more than competent to handle whatever growth her company needed in order to deliver on this deal. She had offices, could manage the increase in staff, and had secured a deposit for the work, thereby mitigating the cash-flow issues. Eventually, we came to the nub of the issue.

Allon: Your only remaining valid fear is that you won't deliver. You're concerned that the campaign won't succeed?

Rachel: Yes!

Allon: Do you think the idea is great?

Rachel: Yes, but who knows?

Allon: Who knows?

Rachel: What do you mean? That's what I asked you.

Allon: Who knows how to do it better than you? Who else in this city has done the amount of retail promotions, retail packaging and in-store promotions that you have?

Rachel: No one that I can think of, offhand. But, maybe someone does know better than me. I'm not arrogant enough to say that I'm the best.

Allon: That's a fair point. Let me ask you this. Do you think anyone deserves it more than you?

Rachel: What do you mean by 'deserves it'?

It was a fair question and the best way I could answer it was by way of a story. And so I told Rachel about Keith, an entrepreneur friend of mine, who runs a little coffee shop and does small catering jobs on the side. He was recently asked to cater for a huge function – much larger than anything he had ever done previously. He was asked to do it because the event organisers had recently sampled his food and loved it. They wanted him to do the job. He turned it down because he believed that they needed to ask somebody 'bigger' to do it. Given his current resources, he thought he could not handle such a big event. What he did not appreciate is that all the 'bigger' people had once been 'small'. At some point, they withstood the competency crisis and took the leap to 'big'. Of course, given his current resources, he could not handle the job. But that was not the point. A 50 per cent deposit on a job of that size would have more than adequately allowed him to put in place everything he needed for a successful large-scale event. So, the job went to someone big and he lost out on the opportunity to shine, to impress and to get a second big job, and a third. He still runs his little coffee shop and remains envious of the big guys. He still thinks they deserve it more than he does.

I paused to allow Rachel to see the connection between the story of Keith and her question, before continuing. 'In my opinion, you and Keith, like many entrepreneurs, need to understand your belief system about your own worth. You somehow think that other people have the right, or are entitled, to success and wealth. In your mind, success and real wealth are for others; they are not for you. But there is no one more entitled to do the big jobs than you. Lorraine has given you the job. She believes you are entitled to it. Now it is up to you to internalise that belief for yourself.'

Rachel paused briefly, took a deep breath and replied, 'You're right. I do deserve it!'

I breathed a sigh of relief. It was essential that Rachel begin to believe in her own worth. Without this belief, she would not be able to grow her business. My relief, it seemed, was short-lived, as Rachel suddenly asked, 'Even if I know I deserve it and even if I believe that no one knows better than me, what if my designers aren't good enough?' And so I went back to questioning her:

Allon: How much influence do you have over who you select to work for you on this project?

Rachel: It's completely up to me. I have total control.

Allon: Exactly! So, you need to hire people who are even better than you! You need to find talented people who are capable of over-delivering.

Rachel: And I will.

Allon: Great! No one has more right to this than you. You found the client. You pitched for the work. You know what you are doing. You are worthy of this work. There are no 'other people' who deserve it more than you. When you internalise that belief and see yourself as the rightful and deserving recipient of the work, and the ensuing wealth, you will rid yourself of the competency crisis. It's time to step up, Rachel!

Rachel: You're right, it is time to step up.

As I was speaking, I could see tears welling up in Rachel's eyes. The reality of the deal, and her facing the competency crisis, may have been a bit overwhelming for her. Despite the bravado of her last statement, I sensed that there was still a lot of fear bubbling beneath the surface. Her tears were not only normal, but healthy. Emotion is not to be feared. I comforted her as best I could and assured her that we still had a long way to go. I was confident that Rachel could manage the contradictions inherent in the journey of an entrepreneur.

The competency crisis usually occurs just after entrepreneurs secure a game-changing deal. The way out of the competency crisis is to work out precisely what will change, or what needs to change, as a result of the anticipated growth of the business. It is a case of facing your fears head-on and working out logically (i.e. not in an emotionally irrational way), why you would not be able to manage the difference between the status quo and the expanded business.

My experience has shown me that the competency crisis is essentially about the fear of not being able to deliver.

If this is indeed the case, then you need to ask what you would need to do in order to ensure not only delivery, but over-delivery. Thereafter, you need to build a strategy around mustering these resources. Work out what you need and begin getting it.

Starting a business is a scary thing. Yet entrepreneurs who are experiencing the competency crisis have already, by virtue of the fact that the business exists, faced some of their fears and sufficiently built their businesses. All they need to do now is build the business more. Whether your business was built by design or by happenstance, you must have had an ability to implement it. Now, at the moment of growth, you are being asked to do it again – but on a larger scale. You are being asked to do it because you are the perceived expert, you know what needs doing. Letting fear stop you is not an option. What is required is real belief that you deserve the growth.

Checklist for Chapter 5

Are you experiencing the competency crisis?	
Are you 'acting as if'?	
Can you hold it together on the way to success?	
Can you visualise future scenarios?	
Can you begin acting in a way that is commensurate with these future scenarios?	
Can you subject your competency crisis to a reality test?	
Do you *really* believe that you deserve success?	

CHAPTER 6

Are you thinking big enough?

Your attitude to growth

By the time Steve arrived, arms laden with bags of Nando's chicken, chips and salads, we were ravenous.

We unpacked the bags and, as we began eating, Steve and I chatted casually – about nothing in particular. It was obvious to both of us that Rachel was deep in thought. Despite attempts to include her in the conversation, she seemed distracted, almost not present. Eventually, Steve asked her what he had missed that morning.

As Rachel began explaining our preceding conversation, it was apparent that she had taken to heart the fact that 'act as if' is an inevitable part of the entrepreneur's journey.

Steve interrupted Rachel's monologue with the question, 'What do you mean by "act as if"?' he asked.

Rachel looked at me as if to say, 'You explain it.'

As I had done earlier in the day, I explained to Steve that when entrepreneurs 'act as if' they are able to put themselves into a future state of success and then make their decisions, regardless of the present state, as if the future existed. Steve did not seem convinced by my explanation. And so I continued, 'The bottom line is that success breeds success. A client's confidence in a business is all about perception. A business that presents a successful image, even if this is imagined, will inspire confidence in the clients, who will perceive the business as being able to deliver. The illusion of success is one of the ways that entrepreneurs manifest success.' By way of example, I explained to Steve and Rachel how I had built processes and created systems for a much bigger Raizcorp – long before the actual need existed. 'I acted as if we were big long before we actually were big. When "big" came, I was ready. In my mind, we had been big all along. Time just had to catch up with me!'

Rachel was quick to jump in before Steve could interrupt further. She had bought into the need to 'pretend'. 'I know I can do it,' she said. 'In fact, I'm excited, but I'm just so scared.'

'What are you scared of?' Steve asked her.

Rachel began talking of her fears, of the increased overheads and larger responsibilities, and of needing to pretend that her business was bigger than it actually was. Steve listened patiently but, suddenly, he interrupted her. 'I don't understand. Isn't this what you've always wanted?' he asked. 'Haven't you been telling me for years how big you wanted Divine Designs to get?'

'I know, I know, I know,' she said, her hands holding either side of her head. Her anguish was palpable. 'I can see it in my mind,' she said. 'Intellectually, I get it, but right now, as we're sitting here, I'm thinking about how I'm going to pay the rent and salaries this month.'

Although I knew that Rachel was scared, the amount of self-doubt that she was now expressing, since Steve had arrived, floored me. I felt sure that I had just convinced her of her own worth. I suddenly felt *myself* plagued by self-doubt. Perhaps I was not as effective a guide as I had believed.

'I'm getting a mixed message here,' I said. 'According to Steve, you want the company to be really big, maybe even international. And yet you're too scared to take the leap of growth presented by your first seriously big client. Which is it?'

'Dreaming is one thing,' said Rachel. 'How can I even think about growing when – after four years – I still battle to pay the bills?'

'I guess you have to decide what you want,' I said. 'According to Steve, you want to be a "growth entrepreneur". Listening to you speak, however, it sounds like you're happy being a "lifestyle entrepreneur".'

'I've never really understood the difference,' said Rachel. 'In my mind, anyone building a business is a growth entrepreneur.'

'In a way, you're right,' I replied. 'Even a lifestyle entrepreneur has to grow their business to a certain point before they have the money to support their lifestyle. The difference really lies in your attitude to growth. Whereas lifestyle entrepreneurs build a business in order to create and maintain a certain lifestyle, growth entrepreneurs continue to grow their businesses indefinitely.'

'My attitude to growth is simple,' said Rachel, smiling. 'It terrifies me!'

Steve and I both laughed.

'It terrifies most entrepreneurs,' I said. 'But, you know as well as I do that fear is no reason *not* to do something. The reality, Rachel, is that, with this deal, Lorraine has bought into *you* as an individual. She is giving you the work because she believes in *your ability* to do the work. And that is how most successful entrepreneurs – whether growth or lifestyle – begin their climb towards the top.'

I continued by explaining to Rachel that very few entrepreneurs know, when they start a business, whether they are a growth or a lifestyle entrepreneur. The 'decision' is something that comes later. It is a function of success. The deal with SWEAT was presenting Rachel with the ability to begin making the decision. Essentially, the question facing her and other entrepreneurs at this point is 'How big do you want this thing to get?'

'What you will now have to decide,' I explained, 'is whether you wish to continue selling *yourself* to clients or whether you will use this opportunity to begin building the value proposition of your business. In this way, in time, clients will not be buying into you, as an individual, any longer – they will be buying into your business.'

'So, basically, you're saying that right now I am the business. The question is whether I want to change that or not,' said Rachel.

'Do you want to?' asked Steve.

'When I think about Carlos at the fruit shop, he's there every day – including Saturdays and Sundays. He's grown his business but he still does not trust anyone else to manage the store. And he told me that he's not interested in opening another shop because his staff would just steal from him! The other day, as I watched him serving a customer, I thought to myself, I don't want to be like him. I want more. I want to employ people to do what I do, hopefully people who can do it even better than me.'

'That's exactly the thinking of a growth entrepreneur,' I said. 'The deal with SWEAT will allow you to employ people and to begin putting in place systems, processes and products that will, slowly, transfer the value proposition from yourself to the business. In time, Divine Designs will be much bigger than Rachel.'

'It's hard to see that now,' said Rachel.

'Sure it is,' I said, 'but it's exciting and, when you begin to see the possibilities that growth will bring, you will replace your fear with the energy of anticipation. The secret is to start thinking big.'

'That's easier said than done,' said Rachel. 'It almost sounds like something you find in a fortune cookie!'

The 100-employee thought experiment

Rachel had a point and so I asked her to indulge me in what I call the '100-employee thought experiment'. I asked Rachel to close her eyes and to begin imagining what her business would look like when she had 100 employees. I gave her some time to begin visualising what, right now, seemed like an impossibility, and, as she allowed her mind to take her to the future, I guided her with some questions. 'When you have 100 employees, how big would your offices need to be? What would be the different departments in the business? Who will your clients be? What will your annual turnover be? Would you have a management team? If so, how many people would be in the team? How much would you be earning?'

As I was asking Rachel the questions, I was also writing them on the whiteboard. After a few minutes, I asked her to open her eyes. As she opened them, and surveyed the questions on the board, a broad smile crossed her face.

- When you have 100 employees, how big would your offices need to be?
- What would be the different departments in the business?
- Who will your clients be?
- What will your annual turnover be?
- Would you have a management team?
- If so, how many people would be in the team?
- How much would you be earning?

'That was fun. The picture wasn't very clear,' she said. 'But it was fun anyway,' she added.

'That's OK,' I said. 'The first step is to begin imagining the growth, and to believe in your ability to make it happen. The second step is to start working it out. So tell me this – what are all the roles you currently fulfil at Divine Designs?'

'What do you mean by "roles"?' asked Rachel.

'Can you tell me all the different functions you're fulfilling on a daily, weekly and monthly basis?'

'You mean like selling?' asked Rachel.

I nodded my head and wrote 'sales' on the board.

'What else do you do?' I asked.

'Wow!' said Rachel. 'What don't I do? I do the designs. I manage the suppliers. I process the invoices and, if I'm feeling really brave, I call the clients for outstanding money.'

'Who manages Mark?' I asked.

'I do, of course,' said Rachel.

I then asked Rachel who paid the suppliers, to which she once again replied that she did.

'What about the books?' I asked Rachel. 'Who does those?'

'At last!' said Rachel. 'Something I don't do. Ivy does the books. She also answers the phone and greets guests.'

Steve had been quiet for a long time. 'Where are you going with this?' he asked. From his tone, he was clearly getting annoyed by the process.

'It's quite simple, actually,' I explained. 'With the exception of design work done by Mark, under Rachel's instruction, as well as Ivy's two roles as bookkeeper and receptionist, Rachel fulfils every role in the business. Almost all these roles will, in time, need to be handed over to employees. And if the business continues to grow, the roles even have the potential to become a fully-fledged department. When I started Raizcorp, if you had told me that, one day, we would have a human resources manager, let alone an HR department, I would have laughed at you. I interviewed, I hired, I approved leave, I trained and I fired. Now, we have an HR department and I have little to do with any of those things. Departments are effectively groupings of the same types of roles. Right now, Rachel, you are the finance department. In time, you will have a finance department that may very well consist of a debtors' clerk, a creditors' clerk, a bookkeeper, an accountant – you may even have a financial director. The question really is, how big do you want this to get?'

I paused before concluding. 'Effectively, a big business is nothing more than a bigger small business.'

'A bigger small business,' said Steve. 'I never thought about it like that.'

'But that is exactly what it is,' I said, glad that Steve appreciated the significance of this realisation.

'I think of it as a foetus growing,' I explained. 'Growth is the result of cells splitting. One cell becomes two, which become four, which become eight and so on. Eventually, the different cells become specialised cells and then they become organs. The departments are simply the organs of your business. Right now, Rachel, you are the heart, lungs and brains of your business. But the baby wants to grow and you are going to have to get out the way!' I said.

'Do you mean I'm going to have to stop designing?' she asked.

'Absolutely!' was my emphatic response. 'Over time, you will need to do less and less of the "doing" work and more and more of the "managing" work. And, eventually, you will even stop the managing work in order to be finding and securing new opportunities to fund the growing business. What you can't do is wait and let the growth take you by surprise. You need to start working it out while you're growing.'

'I'll never stop designing!' she said. 'But I still believe I'm a growth entrepreneur. I'll design and grow.'

I didn't want to argue with Rachel. Perhaps she would find a way to do both. But, in my experience, very few entrepreneurs manage to grow substantial businesses while holding on to the technician role. For now, however, it was clear that Rachel was excited by the prospects of growth.

Although much work lay ahead, I was beginning to hope that Rachel's answer to the question of whether to give up or not was shifting towards the latter.

When growth entrepreneurs allow themselves to imagine the possibilities of growth, they begin to get energised and excited. In this way, the excitement takes over the fear, allowing the entrepreneurs to begin plotting the course towards growth.

Real growth begins when the entrepreneur starts to shift the value provided to the client from himself to others within the business. Growth in Rachel's business will occur when other designers are doing the work, instead of Rachel.

At this point, the value proposition will not reside in Rachel, but within her business. She will be able to attract clients based on the business's ability to deliver, not her own personal ability. This is the secret to growth. In talks and workshops I often ask the audience to name the CEO of Coca-Cola Global. As it turns out, no one can. And yet, almost all of them have enjoyed a Coca-Cola product in the last month. Does anyone care who the CEO is? We don't. As long as the company delivers a quality product, at the right place, at the right price, at the right time, and in the right quantity, we are happy to buy from them. The truth is that Coca-Cola was also once just a one-man band.

When you understand that a big business is simply a bigger small business, you can begin to lessen the fears that accompany the prospects of growth. All businesses, no matter what their size, are essentially doing the same things: we all have customers; we're all adding value and charging our clients for the added value. What changes as a business grows is that the degrees of complexity increase as you add more people to manage the growth and deliver to your clients. Most entrepreneurs that I've dealt with just do not understand this reality.

As part of a business's growth, the entrepreneur will, of necessity, have to slowly give up many of the roles they play in the business. Usually, the best place to start is with the roles at which they are least competent or those roles that take up too much time, for the least gain.

Successful growth entrepreneurs understand this and so they begin planning these handovers, as well as the further splitting of functions, in advance of actual growth.

In his book The E-Myth Revisited, *Michael E. Gerber, who shaped much of my thinking on the way to build a business, distinguishes between three phases through which growth entrepreneurs need to travel if they are to grow their businesses. To paraphrase Gerber's growth phases:*

- *The owner is the doer in his business. This is the 'technician' phase.*
- *As the business grows and he employs people to do the work, he moves to the 'manager' phase.*
- *Ultimately, as his managers grow in competence and the business grows, he can become the 'entrepreneur'. At this point, the business is functioning relatively independently of the owner, who is then free to truly grow the business by networking, marketing, increasing sales and seeking new opportunities for the business.*

According to Gerber, '… it's a three-way battle between the entrepreneur, the manager, and the technician'.[3]

123

Obviously, as business owners move from one phase to the next, they seldom relinquish the previous role completely. Ideally, in Gerber's model, the entrepreneur creates a business so smooth, so systemised, and so independent of its founder, that it becomes possible to sell. Because the business is now independent of its founder, its value is maximised.

While I respect and admire Gerber, and have based a lot of my strategy on his work, in my experience the owner must never completely relinquish either the technician or manager role. Losing touch with the daily workings of the business may leave it vulnerable to bad strategic decisions based on insufficient information. Business strategists speak of the need for CEOs to continue to be 'plugged in' i.e. be involved in both the big picture (i.e. strategy), as well as the details (i.e. operations). I believe that this is good advice for entrepreneurs too as their business grows and becomes more complex.

It's about scale

'So, can we move ahead on the understanding that you are a growth entrepreneur?' I asked Rachel.

She hesitated before answering.

'When I hear you talk and I allow myself to dream, I feel, somewhere deep inside me, that I want it. I just have no idea, even after your whole explanation, how to make it happen. It seems like a bridge too far.'

'That's fine,' I said. 'That's why I'm here. I too have struggled to cross the same bridge but I've seen lots of entrepreneurs find a way to cross it. Effectively, what you need to learn is how to scale your business.'

'What do you mean?' asked Rachel.

'"Scale" simply means multiplying its size,' I replied.

'That's all very well,' said Rachel, 'but at the moment my business consists of three people. I don't even know how to get to ten, let alone a hundred, people. I can barely afford to keep Mark, never mind employ nine or ninety-nine more people!'

I understood Rachel's vacillation between fear and excitement. I reassured her that this was normal for entrepreneurs, at the precipice of growth. On an intellectual level, they fully understand what they are hearing. However, on a deep emotional level they have not, as yet, completely processed their fear. The fear never goes away completely. Some experts even believe that the fear is important for entrepreneurial survival. Success as an entrepreneur comes through managing this fear in a rational way. I explained to Rachel that acceptance of the fear is an important part of the journey. In time, both the frequency and the depth of the fear would change. In my experience, both would decrease. The important thing is to keep going; resilience is, after all, a characteristic of all successful entrepreneurs.

'So, what you're saying is that Rachel just has to keep growing, keep employing, and keep shedding roles?' asked Steve.

'That is what I'm saying. There is, however, one very important factor that cannot be overlooked,' I replied.

'Growth can only occur if the business is in a market that can absorb the scale that Rachel wants to achieve.'

'Can you say that in English?' Rachel asked.

Both Steve and I laughed. 'What I mean is that, first, you have to ask yourself whether the market is big enough for the size of business you wish to create.'

'In other words, is she fishing in a lake full of fish?' asked Steve. 'That's a no-brainer. There's certainly no shortage of retailers.'

'Precisely,' I said. 'Not only that, but there is also no shortage of businesses selling their products through retailers. As far as I am concerned, Rachel is offering a service for which there is a glut of customers. And that brings us to the next question that needs to be asked: does this market want what you are offering?'

Rachel did not hesitate before answering. 'So far, so good,' she said. 'I have small and large retailers interested in my services.'

'Perfect,' I said. Rachel's confidence was growing and I was glad that she was able to acknowledge that the market not only recognised her value, but also desired what she had to offer. Too often, entrepreneurs forget that growth is not possible if they do not have clients who perceive value in their offering – and are prepared to pay for it.

'So you have a market, and the market wants, and will pay for, what you are offering. The next step is to keep offering your clients additional value. So, you need to spend sufficient time ensuring that you are constantly adding value to your products and services. Keep iterating,' I said.

'That's a new one on me,' said Steve. 'What's "iterating"?'

I explained that 'iteration' is a computer term to describe a constantly repeated operation or process, and that entrepreneurs need to do the same thing with their products. They cannot rest on their laurels.

I turned to Rachel. 'You use graphic-design software that is constantly being upgraded. Each iteration adds more and more value to your business, thereby improving your ability and efficiency to deliver to your clients. You need to do the same with your own products. You must keep adding value. That is one of the secrets of success and growth. Your clients come to you for a packaging design and soon you offer them a point-of-sale design solution, and then you add the ability to manage promotions, and suddenly you are the preferred provider for all their retail promotion needs.'

She nodded and I asked her, 'With so many graphic-design programmes on the market, how come you choose to stay with the brand you use?'

'Because nobody else offers the functionalities they do, their backup support is great and I'm used to it,' she replied. 'Also, their software was the first that converted easily between PC and Mac, which saved a lot of time because we could send bug-free files to our printers.'

'Exactly!' I said. 'They have differentiated themselves

in the market, thereby ensuring that you remain a loyal, paying customer.'

'Surely others have copied them?' asked Steve.

'They have,' said Rachel, 'but only much later.'

Steve's question was opportune and so I explained, 'By constantly adding value, they have differentiated themselves, but they have also made it harder for their competitors to copy them.'

I paused, before saying, 'Right now, Rachel, there is nothing stopping anyone from opening up Diviner Designs.'

Both Rachel and Steve laughed, but it was a serious point and so I said, 'The final step in scaling is to protect yourself from your competition.'

'How do I do that?' asked Rachel.

'As a business, there are many ways to protect yourself. Some companies have patents, others build a brand and some use first-to-market strategies. In my opinion, the simplest way for you to protect Divine Designs is, firstly, to specialise – which we've discussed. Then, you need to develop your own intellectual property and then you begin to dominate the market you have created.'

'How do I create intellectual property?' she asked.

'Intellectual property is essentially the synthesis of your experience and knowledge of your industry into processes, systems and products that you may choose to legally protect or not,' I explained.

'Wow! There's more to scaling a business than I thought. It's scary, but it's also exciting,' said Rachel.

'Of course it is,' I said, 'but you can do it. It requires a lot of action. But before action comes thinking – a lot of thinking! And we'll talk about that next.'

Once again, it had been a long session and a break was in order. I had a few things to attend to in my office and so I excused myself. I told Steve and Rachel that I would be back in about fifteen minutes. They seemed more than happy for the time out.

> *The dilemma that many entrepreneurs face is that, although they may have the characteristics of a growth entrepreneur, they don't actually know how to grow and scale their business. There are six fundamental conditions (or ideal states) for scaling a business:*
>
> - *A big enough market exists. One cannot scale a bank if people don't need financial services. It is the basic rule of business: you have to have a market that needs or wants your product. You cannot scale a business without clients to support the size of the business.*
>
> - *The clients must perceive value in the offering. If they do not perceive value, they will not buy your products or services in any significant volume.*
>
> - *Thereafter, even if they perceive value, the clients must have the means, as well as be prepared, to pay for the product.*

- *The product or service needs to be constantly upgraded and improved. It must also remain relevant to an ever-evolving market. This is the 'value-add' condition.*
- *The product must be clearly differentiated from its competitors, and remain so as competitors begin to copy it.*
- *The entrepreneur must put in place the means to protect the product or service from imitation.*

Checklist for Chapter 6

Are you a lifestyle entrepreneur?	
Are you a growth entrepreneur?	
Have you done the 100-employee thought experiment?	
Are you ready to start giving up some of the roles you play?	
What percentage of your time is spent as: • a technician? • a manager? • an entrepreneur (or new-opportunity seeker)?	
What do you need to start doing to move out of the technician role?	
What do you need to start doing to move into the managerial role?	
What do you need to do in order to become the entrepreneur in your business?	
Is the market for your product or service big enough?	

Do you have clients who perceive value in your offering?	
Do these clients have the means, and are they prepared, to pay for the product?	
Are you constantly upgrading and improving your product (adding value)?	
Is the product clearly differentiated from its competitors?	
Have you put in place the means to protect the product or service from imitation?	

CHAPTER 7

What are you missing?

It's not easy till it's easy!

When I returned to the boardroom, Steve and Rachel were sipping coffee. Steve was talking quietly to Rachel. I sensed that he had something he wanted to say.

'What's up?' I asked him.

'I think all of this is easier said than done,' he said.

'At last,' said Rachel, 'someone who agrees with me.'

Since our last conversation, Rachel had been looking a bit shell-shocked. She was clearly feeling quite intimidated by the task that lay ahead of her if she was to scale her business.

'Actually, I agree with Steve as well,' I was quick to reply. 'The fact is, I've done what I'm asking you to do. So, even though I know that it can be done, I'm not, for a second, underestimating the challenge. But – and I think it's very important that you know this – it's no different from any other new challenge. It only seems difficult because you don't know how to do it. Think about learning to drive a car. Today, you get in, start the car and off you go. You don't give a second's thought to steering or changing gears. But, when you first started to learn, it seemed almost impossible to do everything at once. Building the value of a business is no different. Until you have gone through the process of learning how to do it, it will remain difficult.'

'So how does Rachel learn how to cope with this new challenge?' asked Steve. For the first time that day, he was speaking for her. He obviously sensed the overwhelming fear that was pervading the room.

I had, of course, been exactly where Rachel now found herself. 'Are you ready for another story?' I asked.

'Sure,' said Rachel. 'So long as I can just listen and not think too hard, I'm good. My brain feels as if it is going to explode.'

Who's your Hunter Thyne?

So I recounted what I have come to call the 'Hunter Thyne story'. It is a strange name for what was to become a decidedly strange, albeit pivotal, time in my life, as well as in my business. This is the story that I told Steve and Rachel that day.

In 2005, Raizcorp was in serious trouble and I did not know how to fix it. I kept on asking myself what I was doing wrong. In despair, I turned, as I usually do, to my mentor, who uttered the two words that would prove to be my saving grace. 'Go away!' he commanded. By this, he did not mean 'get out of here' – he meant for me to take a break. He suggested that I needed to create distance between myself and the business and that, more than anything, I needed time to think. He generously offered me the use of his holiday home in the quiet seaside town of Sedgefield.

I packed my car, complete with large sheets of white flip-chart paper, coloured markers and Prestik. I intended to take my break very seriously! After arriving at the house, I unpacked and went for a quick swim in the sea. Then I stuck the paper all over the walls of the lounge. This would be my canvas for the next few days and I was convinced that I would find a way out of the financial impasse I was experiencing.

Every morning, I woke up, went for a run and a swim, came back to the house, made breakfast and then I just stared at the paper. I found myself unable to write anything down. I was completely paralysed. I literally sat and stared at white paper until, not being able to stare any more, I found something else to do, anything but think about the business. And so it continued for six days. On the seventh day, I came back from my run and, without a second's thought, I picked up a marker, drew a circle in the middle of a page and inside the circle I wrote a name:

At this point in the story, Steve interjected, 'Hunter who?'

'Hunter Thyne,' I said. 'It's the name of a real person.'

'And who was Hunter Thyne?' asked Rachel.

I promised that all would be revealed as I continued the story.

Implausible as it may sound, Hunter Thyne was a hitch-hiker whom I picked up one afternoon many years ago, as I drove from university in Pietermaritzburg to Durban. We hit it off on the drive and, while we had not remained in serious contact since, we continued to sporadically bump into each other. I think I had probably seen him about five times in the seventeen years between picking him up and his name popping into my head that day.

I have no idea why his name came to me just then, but somewhere in the quiet, in the jogging and the swimming, in the 'non-thinking, non-working' space, perhaps I had seen a hitch-hiker and, without even knowing it, Hunter's name had entered my subconscious. I will never truly know why or how this happened. But there it was – the only thing I had to show for seven days of being away! As I packed the car to return home, I could not help reflecting on the fact that these seven days had been an utter waste of time. When I got back, my wife could see by my face that, although I had returned with a tan, that seemed to be the only thing that had changed. I was still miserable and still believed that I was unable to fix my business.

But, desperate to try anything by this time, I decided to call Hunter. I looked for his card and telephoned him. After a few minutes of small talk, I recounted the story of my week away, and how his name had been the only outcome of my stay. If I had even the tiniest flicker of hope that my efforts would produce a result, Hunter's response definitely extinguished that. He chuckled, thought I was mad and, after exchanging the obligatory 'we must get together' statements, we terminated the phone call. My despair was now complete.

I continued to mope around, doing whatever I could to pursue leads. Exactly three weeks after my phone call to Hunter, on a Sunday morning, the phone rang and it was Hunter. He told me to expect a call from someone at a large bank who was looking to build a business incubator. He did not give me details, just said that he had met this person, the topic of business incubation had come up, and he had immediately thought of our phone call. We both laughed. And, even though I put down the phone excited, a little voice in my head told me that this could not possibly be happening; the synchronicity seemed too far-fetched even by my standards of credulous faith in the ways of the universe.

But it was happening and on Monday, as Hunter had said, the phone call came. Mr Vundla, the head of new products at one of South Africa's 'big four' banks requested a meeting with me. At the meeting, which took place that week, I was told that the bank was prepared to pay me to research and put together a document on what it would take for them to build a business incubator. Hunter Thyne had recommended me as an expert in entrepreneurship and incubation, and so they asked me to submit a quote for the research and compilation of the research proposal. After the meeting, I met with a colleague who I knew would probably be able to help me with the project. We did some maths and presented the bank with a proposal to do the research and write the paper for the princely sum of R250 000. It was more money than I had ever seen at one time. I had envisaged this figure as an opening gambit, a starting point to begin negotiations; never in my wildest dreams did I expect it to be an acceptable offer. Mr Vundla did not blink.

We wrote the paper and we got paid. That money allowed me to pay debt and salaries for the next few months. But, most importantly, it was the confidence booster I desperately needed at the time. Moreover, it led to more work from the same bank, as well as allowing me to approach other banks for work. The additional income allowed me to do more marketing, which resulted in more partner clients. It set the ball of Raizcorp's growth in motion. Who would have guessed that my random decision, to offer a stranger a lift, would have the ability to unblock my path to success seventeen years later?

Quiet and action

'That's all very Zen,' said Steve.

'I like Zen,' said Rachel.

'Zen or not, it's true,' I quickly interrupted. 'The point is that there is great power in giving yourself the opportunity to quieten your mind and just allow thoughts to bubble to the top. As bizarre as it sounds, you need then to act on whatever messages come through. My call to Hunter was nonsensical – I had nothing to ask him or tell him. I simply trusted the power of my subconscious mind to send messages to my conscious mind. And then I took action. The purpose was only revealed later. I have no idea whether that phone call set off a chain reaction that resulted in his meeting the head of new products. Perhaps he would have met Mr Vundla anyway, but would my name have popped into his head if he hadn't spoken to me recently? I will never know. Over the years, I have trusted this process and acted on all messages, no matter how strange,' I said.

'It's too weird for me,' said Steve.

'I felt exactly the same way,' I said. And it was true. I did. I was reminded of, and described to Steve and Rachel, the look on my pregnant wife's face when I – her depressed, morose husband, with few prospects – told her that I needed to go away, alone. But she let me go.

'Now, you need to do the same for Rachel,' I said to Steve.

'I'm happy for her to go,' said Steve. 'Good luck with getting her to leave her business for a week, though!'

'A week!' said Rachel. 'There's no way I can do that.'

Steve gave me an 'I told you' look. I understood Rachel's reluctance to leave her business for a week. But from the short time I had spent with her assistant, Mark, I knew that he was more than capable of managing the business for a week. I told Rachel this and, despite her initial resistance, between Steve and me, we were able to persuade her to take a 'bigger picture' view. What felt like short-term pain would, without a doubt, result in long-term gain. If she was indeed to grow her business, Rachel had to give herself the gifts of time and space.

I had learnt a lot since the time my mentor had sent me off to his holiday home with the vague instruction to 'think'. But unlike him, I presented Rachel with a much more structured approach, almost an assignment. These are the instructions I gave Rachel. As I spoke, she jotted them down in her notebook:

■ Don't rush yourself. Read through the notes you have written in our meetings. Be patient, don't be critical and just process all the information at a leisurely pace.

■ Give yourself time to just 'be'. 'Open your mind and allow your 'universe' to send you messages. Let your 'Hunter Thyne' message emerge.

■ Lastly, ask yourself a very difficult question: how am I standing in the way of my business?

I could see that Rachel was uncomfortable with the last question. She immediately asked me what I meant. I asked Rachel to accompany me to my office and there, next to my desk, I showed her the little hand-written post-it note that I have on the wall with the simple question: How am I standing in the way of Raizcorp?

I explained to Rachel that the question serves as a continual reminder that it is my thoughts, outlook and paradigms, the way I perceive the world, that are influencing the path of the business. Its success is, therefore, directly linked to my levels of self-awareness. The question keeps me conscious of the irony that, inasmuch as I am the builder, I am also the constrainer. It is only by being self-aware, and overcoming my own paradigms and limitations, that I am able to know when to stand firm and when to get out of the way.

On my desk, I had a box filled with little booklets that I had created for the entrepreneurs at Raizcorp. It is called *My 16 Decisions*. The booklets consist of sixteen blank pages. The entrepreneurs each receive the booklet, and it is up to them to fill in their own decisions aimed at developing themselves and growing their business.

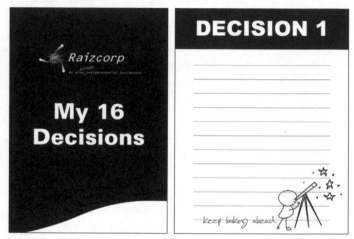

My instructions to Rachel were to take time away on her own and, upon her return, to work through the book with the sixteen decisions that she needed to make – and act upon – in order to unblock the flow and get out of the way of her business's growth.

> *There is a story of a woodcutter whose job is to cut down trees in a forest. He has a certain target to meet. He works very hard, but he is so busy trying to achieve his target that he never takes time to sharpen his saw. Each day it takes him longer and longer to reach his target, and he is exhausted. A passer-by asks him why he does not take the time to sharpen his saw.*

The woodcutter replies that he is too busy working to take the time to sharpen it. What the woodcutter does not realise is that the short time taken to sharpen his saw would save him many more hours of hard work in the future.

This story is often told in the context of time management. For me, there is a far more instructive lesson to be learnt. The entrepreneur's tool is his mind. This is where the business is conceived, and without a sharp mind, growth is unlikely.

Entrepreneurs who do not take the time to sharpen their tools will, like the woodcutter, find themselves exhausted and, ultimately, working far harder than they need for less reward. A sharp mind makes the work easier and the entrepreneur more efficient.

As an entrepreneur, the noise in your head can drown out any rational thought. There is relentless pressure that seems to come from all directions. You may feel that you have no resources left. An entrepreneur, without resources, whether physical, spiritual, mental or emotional, is unlikely to succeed. It is imperative that you give yourself the space and permission to just 'be' and to allow your mind to wander – without judgement and without critical correction.

In this way, you give yourself an opportunity to tap into your powerful subconscious which, in my experience, always produces results.

Rachel's sixteen decisions

Rachel went away for a week to a cottage in the Magaliesberg owned by Steve's father. When we met again, she had already been back in Johannesburg for a week. This time, she was not accompanied by Steve. Having spent a week in the mountains, walking, swimming and, according to her, taking my advice of just allowing herself to 'be', she looked great. She was slightly tanned, had changed her hairstyle and, unusually for her, she was wearing make-up. I immediately asked her how the week away had been.

'I followed your instructions,' she began. 'I really chilled. I read my notes. In fact, I read them twice. For three days I did nothing. I only switched on my phone in the evenings. It was great!

'On the evening of the third day, when I switched on my phone, there was a message from my father,' Rachel said. 'I called him back. That was a big mistake!'

'Why?' I asked her.

Rachel recounted that her father had enquired as to exactly what she had been doing while she was away. She had excitedly explained to him that she was taking time out to plot the growth of her business.

'What did he say?' I asked Rachel.

'He asked me who was looking after the office,' she said. 'When I told him that I had left Mark in charge, he was horrified. He asked me if I was sure I could trust him and then he told me about how his staff used to steal from him. Finally, I heard the sentence I've been hearing my whole life: the only way to do something properly is to do it yourself.'

'How did you respond?' I asked her.

'I was as polite as I could be,' she said. 'But I told him that I would talk to him when I was back and I quickly ended the call. The call infuriated me so much that I immediately took out my booklet and began working on my sixteen decisions.'

With that, she took out the booklet. I could hardly contain my excitement. 'How was the experience of working on the decisions?'

'I loved it,' she said, smiling broadly. 'I was so glad to be alone and to just let my guard down and really look at how right you were about my standing in the way of my own success. It's such a weird concept, but it's true. Even my resistance to going away was illuminating. I always try to find reasons not to do things. It's like even when the opportunity presents itself, I get in the way!'

'Great!' I said. 'Let's get started then. What is Decision 1?'

Decision 1: I need to get away by myself more often.

'The week away was amazing,' Rachel said. 'I really benefited from it. I know that I wouldn't always be able to take a week but three or four days, every now and again, is essential.'

I was happy with what I was hearing. But, in my experience, vague intentions are very different from clear goals. 'How many times a year, and for how long, do you intend going away?' I asked.

Rachel was quiet, obviously mulling over the answer. At last she said, 'I'm going to take three days every four months.'

I was happy with that decision and asked Rachel to write it down in her book as a clear and measurable decision.

It was time to move on to the second decision.

Decision 2: I see Mark as an integral part of Divine Designs' future.

I immediately recognised this as a good decision. In my experience, many entrepreneurs are control freaks. Sharing, letting go and trusting do not come easily to them.

'So, you see a future for Divine Designs?' I asked her.

Rachel merely smiled before continuing. 'The business survived without me. The time away allowed me to see Mark as much more than just a designer. He is as much a part of Divine Designs' future as I am. I want him to be a senior person in the future, if not a partner,' she added.

I congratulated Rachel on the idea, but asked her to reframe the statement so that it was presented as a decision, rather than an idea. She dutifully rephrased the decision:

Decision 2: I see Mark as an integral part of Divine Designs' future.

*Decision 2: I will make Mark a
partner in Divine Designs within 3 years.*

'Let's move on to the third decision,' she said quickly.

*Decision 3: I am changing the
name of the company.*

'That's interesting,' I said. 'What are you going to call it?'

'I'm keeping "Divine Designs", but I'm adding exactly what we do as part of the naming and rebranding. From now on, we will be "Divine Designs: Retail Design Specialists",' she said.

As she continued speaking, the smile on her face was one of pride and accomplishment.

'I realised that I was trying to be all things to all people. Now, when I make a call, or someone asks me what I do, I can tell them, in three words, what we do. Not only that, anyone who sees our name will know exactly what it is we do,' she explained.

I was in complete agreement with Rachel. 'It will also force you to focus on the clients who need that service, thereby reinforcing your specialist status,' I added.

There was no need for me to say anything more. Rachel was clearly on a roll. I was enjoying this meeting immensely!

She turned the page of her booklet to reveal the fourth decision:

*Decision 4: I am going to employ two of
the three freelancers being hired for the
SWEAT project on a permanent basis.*

'That's brave,' I said.

'I know. I feel brave,' she said. 'That's what this decision is about. It's about taking the leap of faith. If I have to pay their salaries, then I will have to bring in the work. And I will,' she added confidently. 'I am going to observe the three of them as we complete this project and, at the end, I will see which two are the best suited to Divine Designs: Retail Design Specialists,' Rachel said, smiling even more broadly now. She clearly got a kick out of saying her company's new name.

Rachel's decision reflected a common entrepreneurial conundrum. The project for SWEAT would give her sufficient income to finance all the designers. However, at the end of the project this income would come to an end. This meant that Rachel would have to start looking for future work now, while the project was still in progress. I explained this to her and added, 'You need to be making plans now to ensure that you will have the cash to pay the salaries of your two new employees.'

It was time for the fifth decision to be revealed:

Decision 5: I am going to stop looking for small jobs worth tens of thousands of rands; instead I will focus on jobs worth hundreds of thousands of rands

I was quick off the mark on this decision.

'What makes you think you can handle these bigger jobs?' I asked.

'In planning for the SWEAT project, and in our meetings, I've learnt that a big job is really nothing more than a bigger small job, with a little added complexity. I can handle it! If I put the right resources and strategy in place, I can manage anything.'

I did not know whether she realised it or not, but Rachel's use of the word 'manage' was instructive. Even from the language she was using, it was clear that she was not seeing herself as a technician in her business any more. This was crucial to her growth. She was stepping into the managerial role and, from there, it would be a natural transition to 'Gerber's entrepreneur'. That was when she would really start to grow her business – even beyond her wildest dreams.

It was time for the sixth decision.

Decision 6: I will perfectly understand my costs for each project.

We had spent a lot of time on the importance of costing and I was glad that Rachel had included this as one of her decisions.

'I'm tired of losing money,' she said. She didn't need to add anything else to this crucial decision.

Decision 7: I will increase my prices by 15% and will not be scared to tell my clients.

'In the week since I've been back, I've been comparing my prices with those of equivalent design agencies,' said Rachel. 'I am at least 20 to 50 per cent cheaper for what I believe is better work.'

'Why is that?' I asked.

'I think I was just afraid to charge market prices in case I didn't get the work. I've been competing by being cheaper and it's got me nowhere. I'm not doing it anymore.'

'Why only 15 per cent?' I asked her.

'I don't think that much more is reasonable,' she said.

'That's bullshit!' I said. 'You have just told me that your competitors are at least 20 to 50 per cent more expensive than you. Remember that you cannot compete on price,' I said.

'Fine!' said Rachel, as she rewrote the decision in her book:

Decision 7:
I will increase my prices by ~~15~~ 20 % and will not be scared to tell my clients.

There was a determination in Rachel's voice that I had not heard for a long time. It was clear that she had made up her mind. I was keen to see the remaining decisions.

Decision 8: I will create products out of my services.

'This is a difficult decision,' said Rachel. 'I have not yet worked out exactly what the products will be, but I realise that I have to package my services in such a way that allows my customers to easily understand what they are getting.'

I nodded in agreement. Cole's Law had clearly had an effect on her. It is crucial that clients know what they are buying. I suggested to Rachel that she work out how many products she would be able to create over the next year. She nodded and noted this in her booklet before we moved on to the next decision.

Decision 9: I will get to know my competitors better.

'What do you mean by that?' I asked. 'Are you going to go for tea with your competitors?

Rachel smiled. 'I'm serious. I've basically ignored my competitors. I intend to do real research on them. I'm going to find out what they are offering, how they price their goods and services and what their differentiators are,' she said.

'How will this help you?' I asked her.

'Well, if I know what they're doing, it will help me to design my products and services better, so that I can better differentiate myself. It's quite simple really,' she said.

Rachel really seemed to be getting it, and I was proud of her. I told her this before we moved onto the tenth decision.

Decision 10: I will improve the quality of my marketing material.

'It's time for me to live my brand,' said Rachel. 'I've always tried to save money on brochures, business cards, even my website. But my business is all about image and I'm projecting the wrong image to prospective clients. I am going to rebrand as soon as possible.'

'Can you afford that?' I asked.

'Well, that's where the next decision comes in,' said Rachel.

Decision 11: I will personally call every client who owes me money.

I smiled again. I was now convinced that Rachel's transformation was real.

'I'm not afraid to ask for money anymore,' she said emphatically. 'I've done the work and then my clients still make me work to get the money they owe me. It's not right! I deserve that money and I'm going to make sure I get it. But I'm also putting in a new payment policy – which is my next decision.'

Decision 12: I will ask for a 50% deposit on all jobs.

'This will increase my cash flow and also reduce my risk,' she said.

Obviously, I was in full agreement with Rachel. I also knew, having learnt my own lessons, that this policy would substantially ease her cash-flow situation. There is a great saying that 'turnover is vanity, profit is sanity, but cash flow is reality'. For small businesses, cash-flow is truly the difference between survival and closure.

Decision 13: I will hold monthly management meetings with my bookkeeper.

'I am so tired of not understanding the finances of my business,' said Rachel. 'It's my business for heaven's sake!' she added.

'That could be your best decision,' I said. 'Not only do you need to have meetings, but you also need to insist on understanding what your bookkeeper is saying.'

'I know that now,' said Rachel. 'It's time for me to understand the difference between an income statement and a balance sheet, as well as the difference between cost of sales and expenses.'

Decision 14: I will find customers outside of Johannesburg.

This was an unexpected decision. Perhaps Rachel saw the questioning look on my face because she was quick to say, 'Don't worry. I'm not getting ahead of myself. But, there's really no reason why I can't promote myself in other places.'

I agreed with Rachel, but warned her against being too ambitious. There can be great value in expanding one's business beyond one's geographical comfort zone. One does, however, have to be prepared for unexpected costs and unforeseen eventualities. But it was a good decision. Too often, entrepreneurs are too short-sighted, only pursuing clients in their own area.

'As long as you can find a way to make it cost-effective, and worth your time and effort, go for it!' I encouraged Rachel.

'Cape Town has so many retailers and head offices of retail companies,' she said. 'I will find a way to make it lucrative,' she said.

The next decision was a complete change of course.

Decision 15: I'm going on a personal development course or workshop.

At Raizcorp we offer a course called 'Who am I?' It is compulsory for all our entrepreneurs in their first year with Raizcorp. Many entrepreneurs focus so much on their business that they lose sight of the most important component of the business – themselves! Self-awareness is one of the keys to growing a business. I believe that entrepreneurs who know what makes them tick are far better prepared to deal with the personal challenges that accompany the journey than those whose self-awareness is limited. I did feel, however, that I needed to caution Rachel against one thing.

'Just ensure that you don't become a workshop "junkie",' I said.

She laughed before responding. 'Don't worry!' she said. 'I know the types who attend every seminar, talk and workshop, and still take no real action. I'll never become one of them. I'll choose carefully. Anyway, with Steve as my husband, I'll never get away with workshop hopping. He's very sceptical of people who offer to change your life in a weekend!'

It was time for the final decision.

Decision 16: I am going to see myself as a salesperson – I need to sell, sell, sell!

Having revealed the final decision, Rachel sat back and said, 'This is where I am going to need the most help,' she said.

'And that is precisely where we will go at our next – and final – meeting,' I said. But there was an elephant in the room and I could not hold back any longer.

'Did you have a "Hunter Thyne moment"?' I asked Rachel.

'I did, but it was not at the cottage,' she said. She paused briefly. 'It happened on the drive home. I was driving along and reflecting on the week. I was so happy that I had completed the sixteen decisions but I also had a nagging feeling because I hadn't had my own "Hunter Thyne moment". But, I just let it go. I was so excited about the decisions and then the phone rang. I looked down. It was my father. I ignored the call and just continued driving.'

As she uttered these words, I saw that tears were welling up in her eyes. Reaching for a tissue, she continued.

'And then it hit me! I'd had my own "Hunter Thyne moment". It just came to me, from somewhere deep in my head. I realised that I would never be able to run this business until I tuned out my father's voice. I have absorbed all his views on how to grow a business. He was definitely a lifestyle entrepreneur who never believed in employing competent people to help him to expand his business. He was a control freak and kept such a stranglehold on the business that he never allowed it to grow beyond a one-man operation for more than a few months at a time. According to him, everyone he employed was either a thief or incompetent, and he ended up firing them. As I continued to drive, I realised that I had been doing the same thing as my father. And so, I made my seventeenth decision. I decided that I was going to switch off my father's voice in my head and become my own type of entrepreneur. I have been standing in the way of my own success by taking on my father's belief system. Without any disrespect to my father, I have decided that it is time to grow up and to grow my business in my own way.'

She sat back and sighed. There were no more tears in her eyes. In their stead were resolution and calm.

At this point, I felt confident that Rachel would not be giving up.

'I'm not afraid to grow the business. I'm sure that I will work out the "how" along the way. What I need help with now is how to find the clients. Perhaps I need to employ a real salesperson instead of doing the sales myself,' she said.

'Employing a salesperson may be a solution in the long run,' I said. 'But right now, you can't abdicate from the sales role. You need to learn to sell your own products and services before you can get someone else to do it. Even then, you must never stop selling. Successful entrepreneurs are always selling.'

It had been a long morning and both Rachel and I were exhausted. The decisions were big and her realisations even bigger. It was time to call it a day. We arranged for one last meeting in two weeks' time. It would not be a long session. I asked Rachel to call my assistant to set up a two-hour meeting. I promised Rachel that we would discuss sales and, thereafter, I trusted that in her arsenal she would have everything she needed to make her ultimate decision.

Nothing you learn or experience during your journey as an entrepreneur will have any effect on your business or your life, until you decide that it can. The word 'decide', from Old French, literally means 'to settle a dispute'.

Entrepreneurs are often in dispute with themselves; they wrestle with the question of 'should I or shouldn't I?' Whatever the dispute, action comes from a decision. Entrepreneurs need to make the decision to think differently and, as a result of the changed thinking, to act differently. It is not about trying harder; it is about taking new actions, new approaches and new pathways. Initially, many of the decisions, and their resultant actions, will feel uncomfortable. They will be unfamiliar. There is a great tendency to revert to the old ways of thinking and acting. One of my favourite quotations, attributed to Alfred A. Montapert, is 'do not confuse motion and progress. A rocking horse keeps moving but does not make any progress'. Indecision is motion; decisions lead to progress.

My colleague Linda Hart, a wise and successful entrepreneurial guide, counsels entrepreneurs to 'give themselves permission'. It is sage advice. Give yourself permission to make your decisions with confidence and to move forward confidently in the direction of your dreams (to quote Thoreau, another wise man).

You can take as long as you like to make these decisions, and as long as you like to put your decisions into effect. Your personal and business transformation cannot happen without them, so trust yourself and decide.

Checklist for Chapter 7

Have you taken time out to just 'be'?	
Is your mind open and receptive to the messages coming your way?	
Have you asked yourself how you are standing in the way of your business?	
Have you made your '16 Decisions'?	
Have you made the decision to think differently and, as a result of the changed thinking, to act differently?	
Are you prepared to take new actions, new approaches and new pathways?	
Have you 'given yourself permission' to do whatever needs doing?	

CHAPTER 8

Sell, sell, sell

What's your story?

As arranged, Rachel and I met two weeks later. I believed that we had arrived at a crucial point in the journey. Rachel's passion for her business had been reignited and her determination and resolve to build the company were apparent. Furthermore, she was on her way to understanding the crucial need to develop products.

Unfortunately, passion and products are not enough to keep a business alive. I was quite emphatic on this point. 'You may have the best product in the world, but if no one knows about it, your business cannot grow. You have to take your product to the target market and sell it to the people who need it,' I said to Rachel. I was quick to add, however, that I am not a sales guru. I have learnt a lot of what I know about sales from reading and courses. I urged her – as I do all entrepreneurs – never to stop learning. There are great books on the subject of selling, as well as DVDs and CDs that can help entrepreneurs to sell, sell and sell.

'From now on,' I said to Rachel, 'selling needs to become your obsession.'

'How do I do that?' she asked.

'Most people don't realise that selling is a process,' I explained. 'The best salespeople know this and are meticulous about following the process. They identify targeted clients, they bring them into a pipeline and then they close the deal. They do this in a planned, step-by-step process.'

Rachel was listening intently and so I went on to explain that the process is different in every business. Some products have a long sales cycle; others have a short one. Some are affected by seasonality; others are not. There are products that are easier to sell to women and there are some products that are easier to sell in the morning!

'What you need,' I said to Rachel, 'is to master the understanding of the sales process in your own business.'

I allowed this point to sink in before continuing. 'You need to start by working out who to target and the best time to call them,' I said.

'You're right,' she said. 'I often call them too late. Retailers do their planning way in advance for special events, such as Easter or Valentine's Day, and by the time I wake up I've already missed the boat!'

'Exactly,' I said. 'You and Mark need to sit down with a calendar, and be looking at least eighteen months ahead. In that way, you can plan not only who to target, but when to target them.'

'I get it,' said Rachel, 'but then what?'

'The next thing you need to do is think through your story,' I said.

'My story?' asked Rachel. 'I thought we were talking about selling. Do you mean my elevator pitch?'

'No, your elevator pitch is your 55-second answer to the question, what does your business do? As we've discussed, in the past, it's very important to have that one down pat. Your story is something else. It's the answer to a different question: why are you in this business? In my opinion, your story is the key to unlocking large sales,' I said. If you intend to scale your business, you need to have a clear, succinct and elegant answer to the question, why are you in this business?'

'Why are you in *your* business?' asked Rachel.

'That's an easy one for me,' I said. 'Someone believed in me and now I do the same for others. Someone paid it forward for me and now I pay it forward for others. That's my story!'

I went on to tell Rachel of an experience I had had recently that beautifully illustrates the power of a story in selling products and promoting a business. I am involved in an entrepreneurial competition called Pitch & Polish, an Idols-type show in which entrepreneurs compete by pitching their businesses to an audience and judges. In the 2011 competition, one of the candidates had developed a range of natural ethnic hair products using avocado oil. In her first pitch, she merely described the product and, based on her pitch, there seemed to be no connection between her and the product. I pushed her to answer the question, why this product? Although reluctant at first, she eventually told us that she had watched her mother, who had used ethnic hair products her whole life, go bald by the age of 60 and how she herself, at only 30 years of age, was beginning to see her hair destroyed by the harsh chemicals in all the ethnic hair products. She knew that there had to be an alternative, and this got her thinking. She lived in an area of South Africa that had a bountiful supply of avocados and had grown up hearing people tell 'old wives' tales' about avocado oil being good for hair. So she began researching the properties of avocado oil and the idea of a product range came to her. When she told *this* story, the audience response began to change completely. She went on to the next round, by which time she had polished the story. The judges and the audience bought it and she went on to win the competition.

'I have little doubt that one of the main things that gave her an advantage over the other finalists was a powerful and personal story that she told well. Her story is what is going to bring investment and promote sales in her products.'

I paused to let this information sink in before asking Rachel, 'So, what is your story?'

She looked at me wide-eyed and I laughed. 'You don't have to come up with it right now,' I said. 'You just have to start thinking about it and, as you develop your products in the next few months, begin to work on a clear and concise answer to the question, why this business?'

Stories are powerful. When it comes to sales and what I call the 'business story', it is not about making up a fictional story.

It is about connecting the dots between seemingly random events in such a way that you connect yourself to your business. The ability to articulate the 'why you?' and the 'why this?' are crucial to the success both in selling your products and promoting your business.

I am not suggesting that entrepreneurs need to fabricate a story. In my experience, almost all successful entrepreneurs have a tale to tell. Both the tale, and the telling of it, needs to capture the imagination of listeners. In that way, the story begins to unlock the relationship between the entrepreneur and potential clients. Bill Gates, Raymond Ackerman and Richard Maponya all have stories; many of us know these, or the stories of other entrepreneurs. It is no surprise that they are successful entrepreneurs. In my opinion, there is a direct link between the story and their success.

What is your story?

Getting out there

'It's all very well to have an elevator pitch and a story,' said Rachel. 'The challenge is to find people who want to listen to me.'

I knew that Rachel was right. But, as an entrepreneur, once you know that your primary responsibility is to sell, sell, and sell, there are definite ways to ensure that you expose yourself to the right people and that you find opportunities to pitch your business, either using your elevator pitch or your story. In the final part of today's discussion I planned to share some thoughts on selling, beyond the obvious textbook stuff that Rachel could read anywhere. Thereafter, she would have to finally answer the question, are you up to it?

Promising Rachel that I would not keep her much longer, I began.

'An obvious place to get exposure is at networking events – both business and social. And you need to attend as many of these as possible. I firmly believe that early-stage entrepreneurs who do not network will not succeed. That has been my experience. When it comes to networking, there are several things to keep in mind.' As I listed my 'tips for networking', Rachel wrote them down in her notebook:

- You need to know your story.

- You need to have an elevator pitch ready.

- You need to listen more than you speak.

- You must always have a supply of business cards with you.

- Most importantly, you must always follow up on leads.

'That doesn't sound too difficult,' said Rachel.

'Networking is not difficult,' I said. 'Especially if you change the way you view it. For me, every networking event is rich in opportunities for random encounters that could lead anywhere. I see the events as an opportunity to connect, to learn and to be inspired. Networking excites and energises me!'

Another key to being comfortable at networking events is to change the way you perceive this thing we call 'selling'. I recounted to Rachel my experience with John Hall, a Raizcorp partner. In a guiding session with John, we discovered that he saw selling as a degrading activity. In his mind, sales activity was the equivalent of begging for work. He felt it to be beneath him. I explained to him that, for me, selling was about telling people about the great work we do. I love telling people about what Raizcorp does. I'm proud of it and it excites me to share it with others. When John began to see selling as a way to tell his story, his ability to attend and feel comfortable at networking events changed. Rather than being intimidated by the thought of networking and whatever fears that term conjures up for her, I suggested that Rachel began to reframe the notion of 'selling' into 'telling her story'.

'I can do that,' she said, seeming quite excited at the prospect.

'There is another opportunity for exposure based on your decision to rebrand your business,' I said. 'Rebranding gives you a great opportunity to communicate with your old clients.'

'Old clients?' she said, looking confused.

'Old clients are such a neglected group of people!' I said. 'Rebranding your company gives you an excuse to call previous clients and reintroduce yourself to them. Busy people easily forget names they don't come into contact with regularly. If the people you dealt with before are still there, this will put your name and your company back in the forefront of their minds. But it may be that the people you dealt with in the past have moved on, and then you have a great chance to promote your business to the new decision-makers.'

Rachel looked intrigued. 'I've really never thought of going back to clients who are no longer using my services. I always think that if I haven't heard from them, they must be getting what they need elsewhere,' she said. 'Also, I'm always looking forward, only thinking about new leads all the time.'

'New leads are obviously very important,' I said. 'You need to focus on both the old and the new. But, when it comes to new clients, the best piece of advice I can give you is to qualify your leads. This means that before you pick up the phone to a new client, you need to have researched who they are and what you perceive their needs to be. If you are lucky enough to secure an appointment, then you need to have a prepared presentation that speaks quickly and clearly to their pain and your ability to resolve it.'

Building your channel

Rachel was taking notes as I spoke so I also mentioned that one of the tricks many entrepreneurs miss is that they don't build their 'channel'.

'What's a "channel"? asked Rachel.

The very question confirmed that Rachel, like many entrepreneurs, did not understand this concept. So I explained that a channel simply refers to people who are able to refer work to you. You build your channel by leveraging off other people's networks, thereby widening your access to all sorts of people and opportunities. The most obvious channel partners are, of course, current clients, because they are able to vouch for you.

'But why would they do it?' asked Rachel.

'Some people do it on a commission basis. And that is perfectly legitimate,' I said. 'Basically, you make agreements with well-networked people so that, if they refer work to you and you are successful in securing a contract, they will get a certain commission. Other times, your channel partners do it to enhance their own offering to their clients.'

I could see that Rachel was unsure of what I meant and so I gave an example. 'Take the guy you use for printing, for instance. He may have clients who he thinks could benefit from your services. If he refers them to you, he is adding value to his own offering to these clients.'

Every business has opportunities to access clients either directly or indirectly. Indirect access is done through channel partners. The benefit of following a channel partner strategy is that one can leverage a one-to-many relationship. This means that every single relationship you have with a channel partner may yield tens, if not hundreds, of potential clients.

Whether you decide to use a commission-based channel model or not, you need to constantly keep your channel partners informed of new products and services.

Communicate with them on a regular basis, through newsletters, events or mails. Recognise them and reward them for their efforts. Microsoft is a great example of a company whose success is largely built on their effective use of channel partners.

Public relations

'Public relations is yet another very potent arrow in the entrepreneur's quiver,' I said. 'And, of course, once you have your story, the media are always looking for content.'

'So what must I do, work out my story and then send it to magazines?' asked Rachel.

'Not quite,' I said. 'When Raizcorp started, I didn't have money for advertising. I believed that if I sent articles to the press about what we were doing, they would automatically get published. Of course, they didn't! The media will only publish your story if it is newsworthy and different, and provides some kind of value for their audience. If you sent an article saying that Divine Designs had become a retail specialist, who would care? You need to find an angle. Journalists are always looking for angles.'

'What sort of angle could I find?' asked Rachel.

I thought for a second before responding.

'For example, if you monitored the success of your deal with SWEAT, and the campaign is a real hit, which we believe it will be, you could quite easily get an article written with the headline: "Small Local Company Makes Big with International Chain".'

'I like the sound of that,' said Rachel.

'Exactly!' I said. 'And so will readers. Some of the readers will be potential clients. Add a quote by Lorraine, SWEAT's marketing manager, and you have credibility. That's the value of good PR.'

I told Rachel about Angel Jones, who founded Homecoming Revolution, an organisation dedicated to bringing expatriates back to South Africa and helping them find employment. Angel Jones (née Angela Jones) appears in public with angel wings attached to her back. It has become her trademark. I have little doubt that this has made her something of a celebrity and contributed to Homecoming Revolution's ability to appear in the media – without ever having to advertise.

'I have to warn you, however, that PR requires a certain level of maturity,' I said.

'What do you mean by that?' asked Rachel.

'That the minute you believe what is written about you, you're in trouble,' I said.

Sensing that Rachel was unsure of what I was talking about, I continued.

'One of the problems with positive PR is that it can inflate your ego to such an extent that you lose touch with reality. This is what happens to the "do you know who I am? CEOs". Often, when they are the flavour of the month, they start believing the hype that is written about them and they become arrogant. For many, pride really does come before the fall. The flipside of that, of course, is negative PR. The reality is that, with the plethora of social-media platforms available today, it is very easy for people to criticise you. You need to take both the good and the bad with a proverbial pinch of salt. Deal with constructive criticism but don't believe everything they say about you – whether it is positive or negative. The other thing about PR is that some entrepreneurs fall in love with it. They then begin to pursue the PR possibilities to the detriment of building their company. Don't prioritise radio interviews and the media circuit over selling products and building your business,' I warned Rachel.

'I should be so lucky!' said Rachel, laughing.

I gave a knowing smile. If someone had told me when I began to seriously pursue Raizcorp's growth that I would be turning down interview opportunities, I would also have laughed at them. However, if you are serious about building a business, you will find that with success come the opportunities to publicise the success. Too often, falling in love with the publicity is the beginning of the downward slope. I knew that if Rachel began to seriously grow her business, she would become a force to be reckoned with in the retail design world. It was important that I caution her against falling in love with the limelight.

In 1994, I was working in an ailing retail clothes shop in Durban. After many attempts to revive the business, to no effect, I decided I needed to employ desperate measures. The business was going downhill anyway so I had nothing to lose. First I emptied the shop windows. Then I created a promotional flyer that stated: 'Bring in a pair of old shoes and we will give you a R20 discount on any purchase. I had the flyers printed in English and Zulu and we handed them out to passers-by.

It started slowly but then more and more customers began bringing in their old shoes. As each pair arrived, I placed them in the shop window. Passers-by began taking notice and soon they, too, began arriving with their old shoes. Within two months, we had 5000 pairs of shoes in the windows. I decided to try my hand at PR and called a local charity to donate the shoes to them. At the same time, I contacted various newspapers to cover the story, and to witness the handover of the shoes to the charity.

On 18 April 1994, a reporter arrived at the shop to interview me. She also took a photograph of me surrounded by thousands of pairs of shoes ready for donation to charity. On 19 April 1994, the shop received invaluable PR when a large photo and article appeared in the newspaper. It was the beginning of the chain's return to success and profitability. There are PR opportunities everywhere. The secret is to both create and seek out the opportunities.

Remember that everything you say and do is potential PR.

The image you project to everyone you meet is part of your PR campaign. Ensure that you and your business are in the public eye as much as possible.

In the words of Zach Culter, 'while advertising is paid for; publicity is prayed for'. Make sure your publicity is positive!

Thought leadership

The meeting was drawing to a close. There was, however, one more very important and often neglected piece of advice that I wished to give Rachel. It is a realm into which most entrepreneurs never venture. In their minds, it is a space for academics and intellectuals. How wrong they are! I began by asking Rachel a question: 'Do you know what "thought leadership" is?'

'Nope,' was her immediate response.

'Do you remember, a few weeks ago, I had to step out for a radio interview?' I asked. Rachel nodded.

'That was thought leadership in action,' I said. 'They did not call me about Raizcorp. They were calling to ask my opinion on a subject connected to entrepreneurship.'

I told Rachel that, as part of my monthly regime, I think about issues in my field (i.e. small businesses and entrepreneurship) about which I have concerns, and I think through what my views on the subject are. If appropriate, I write an article on the topic, which I send to editors, or alternatively I tweet an opinion on Twitter. In this way, I have consequently positioned myself as a thought leader in my field.

'That's easy for you!' said Rachel. 'You work in a field that is not only topical, it lends itself to thought leadership.'

'Tell me,' I asked Rachel, 'do you think the funeral business lends itself to thought leadership?'

Rachel looked at me aghast. 'No!' was her immediate response.

'Exactly, and yet one of Raizcorp's partner companies, an IT business, of all things, has positioned itself as a thought leader in this field.'

'Now I'm interested,' said Rachel.

I proceeded to tell her about Chris Ogden, the MD of RubiBlue, which is a software-development business. As part of their process of productisation, they developed a software product designed to help funeral homes manage the sales and administration of funeral policies. The product has really become successful and RubiBlue is becoming the preferred provider to what is, unfortunately, a huge growth industry. In the process, Chris has investigated, researched and learnt so much about the funeral industry. While working with Chris, who is a Raizcorp partner, I suggested, just as I had now suggested to Rachel, that he develop a thought leadership platform on the subject.

'He looked at me, the same way you did,' I told Rachel. 'He thought I was mad in the head.'

'And what happened?' asked Rachel.

'I pushed him, just as I have pushed you,' I said, 'and I found out that there are two magazines aimed specifically at the funeral industry. I suggested to Chris that he write an article and submit it to one of the publications.

The article was published, together with a short description of the author, the business, and their contact details. As a result of the article, Chris was invited to speak at a conference. After his talk, he was mobbed by interested people. Opportunities have opened up for him beyond South Africa's borders and, suddenly, Chris Ogden, software developer, is on his way to becoming a thought leader in the world of funeral-policy management.'

'Wow!' said Rachel. 'That's a great story.'

'It is. And you, too, have a great story. I know you started off as a salesperson in a retail store before you became a designer, and now you have your own growing company and are becoming an expert in retail designs. What you need to do is to think through the issues and challenges in your industry, form opinions and write articles. Before you know it, your name will be out there and you'll be in demand.'

I could not have hoped for a broader smile on Rachel's face. If she was willing to put in the hours, do the work and take not only herself but her business to the next level, there was little doubt in my mind that she could become a successful businessperson and a thought leader in her field.

Thought leadership is something that entrepreneurs often neglect. But it is a great opportunity for free publicity. Publications are always looking for content. Provided that the material is credible and well thought through, there will always be an opportunity to get publicity. Presented as thought leadership, publicity builds your credibility in your industry – and that can never be a bad thing!

Thought leadership has recently had some negative publicity of its own, however.

> *Not everyone is a thought leader. Thought leadership is not just about producing random content. This is best described by Craig Badings, who describes himself as passionate about thought leadership, on his website (http://www.thoughtleadershipstrategy. net):'Thought leading content is content that offers new or fresh thinking on a topic. It's not merely peddling an opinion or curating other people's content – it is a new, fresh perspective often based on empirical evidence.'[4]*
>
> *If you have something new to say, ensure that you say it and that it gets out there!*

The two hours had sped by and it was time for us to go to our respective appointments. The Rachel that I was saying goodbye to now was a very different Rachel from the woman who had first walked into the boardroom a few Saturdays ago. She had listened, she had argued, but, ultimately, she had pushed herself to move beyond her own perceived limits. The road ahead would not be easy. The entrepreneurial journey is not about easy; it is about perseverance. And Rachel, like the many entrepreneurs I have the privilege of working with, certainly has an abundance of that quality.

Trevor Waller, my co-writer on this book, likes to compare life to the recording on an ECG machine. Life is quite literally represented by a series of up and down movements. Absence of life is a straight line. The secret to success is to embrace both the ups and the downs of the journey. Do not long for a straight line. When that comes, life is over!

173

Rachel thanked me and I wished her well on her continuing journey. She knew that I would always be there for her. But I hoped that she also now knew that she did not need me. She had all the tools she needed to build a flourishing business! So, too, do you. Good luck!

Checklist for Chapter 8

Do you read books, listen to CDs, watch DVDs and attend talks about selling?	
Have you worked out the sales process for your business?	
Do you know who you are targeting and when is the best time to call them?	
Have you worked out your story?	
Do you have an elevator pitch?	
Do you attend networking events?	
Have you made contact with former clients?	
Have you built a channel of partners?	
Do you create PR opportunities for yourself and your business?	
Have you considered ways in which you could become a thought leader in your industry?	

Epilogue

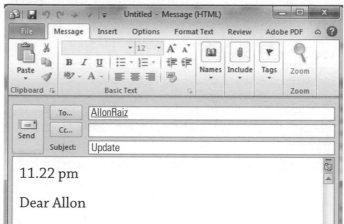

11.22 pm

Dear Allon

I've just walked in from an industry networking event. Your name came up in conversation, and I suddenly realised that it's been three months since our last meeting!

The SWEAT promotion is finally over and I'm really happy to say that it was very successful. Lorraine loved our work and we are already in negotiations for their next promotion! It was definitely not smooth sailing, but Mark really stepped up and, together, we pulled it off. Even though the three designers did what they had to do, I've decided that only one of them is worth employing permanently. Don't worry, my decision to employ two designers still stands. I'm already interviewing potential candidates and I have a clearer idea of what I'm looking for. You will be very proud of me, as

I have developed a test for potential designers to see whether they are able to follow a brief, as well as to gauge their creativity and speed. Putting this system in place means that I only interview people who have the skills that I am looking for. This has really saved me time and allowed me to focus on ... guess what ... sales!

I thought I would really miss being in the design studio, but I've found a hidden talent for performing. I really enjoy presenting the business and our concepts. I have my story and have found that I have more opportunities than ever before to tell people why I do what I do. I must admit that I am still struggling with working out what my 'secret sauce' is but I remember you saying that I need to give it time. I hope one day to tell you that I have it. Just don't ask me to reveal it!

'My 16 Decisions' booklet goes everywhere with me and I'm slowly ticking them off one by one. The rebranding exercise is complete and we will be featured in a marketing magazine next month. But this is not my only PR accomplishment. I'm sure you read the article I mailed you about the SWEAT promotion. The article led to an enquiry from Unilever and we're in the final stages of pitching a campaign to them (much bigger than SWEAT)! So hold thumbs for us please.

I'm doing the costing far more accurately than before, which has really improved our cash flow. Although it's nowhere near where I want it to be, I'm optimistic that we are on our way. I increased my hourly rate by 20 per cent, as discussed, and, as you predicted, we did not lose any clients.

With the SWEAT promotion finally over, I'm taking Steve away next weekend. He has really stood by me and been a tower of strength. There are still days when I think of giving up. But those days are becoming fewer and fewer.

I remember offering to pay you for all the time you spent with me. You said that the best way to pay you back was for me to take what I learnt and apply it to building a successful business. I am not there yet, but payment is on its way!

Onward and upward!

Rachel

PS Expect a call from someone called Robert who I met at the event this evening. His business is taking off and he's battling to deal with the rapid growth.

References

1. Tart, Nick and Scheidies, Nick. *50 Interviews with Young Entrepreneurs: What it takes to make more money than your parents*. Wise Media Group, Denver, 2010.

2. Brotman, Adam. *Act as if*. http://www.adambrot man.com/blog/2012/02/19/act-as-if/. Accessed: March 2012

3. Gerber, Michael E. *The E-Myth Revisited: Why most small businesses don't work and what to do about it*. Harper Business. 1995.

4. Badings, Craig. http://www.thoughtleadership strategy.net. Accessed: March 2012